Africa's Brave Heart

Africa's Brave Heart

Robert Moffat

Irene Howat

CF4·K

10 9 8 7 6 5 4 3 2 1

© Copyright 2014 Christian Focus Publications

Paperback ISBN 978-1-84550-715-2

epub ISBN 978-1-78191-360-4

mobi ISBN 978-1-78191-361-1

Published by Christian Focus Publications,
Geanies House, Fearn, Tain, Ross-shire,
IV20 1TW, Scotland, U.K.
Tel: +44 (0)1862 871011
Fax: +44 (0)1862 871699
www.christianfocus.com
email: info@christianfocus.com

Cover design by Daniel van Straaten
Cover illustration by Jeff Anderson
Printed and bound in Denmark by Nørhaven

Contents

For Isabel, Kenny, Ruth, Alison and Iain

How it all Began

If a boy had to choose where to live for adventure, he might choose Portsoy in Scotland. Robert's family lived there because his father was a Customs Officer and Portsoy was a seaport. Mr Moffat's job was to make sure that the trading done in Portsoy was legal, that nothing illegal was landed or shipped and that all taxes were paid.

'There's nobody more imaginative than a smuggler,' Mr Moffat would often say, 'and nobody more stupid. Sometimes I wonder if they think my brain doesn't work.'

His wife knew that he must have a story to tell about his day's work because he always started his stories by saying exactly the same thing.

'What's been happening?' she asked.

Mr Moffat shook his head. 'I was checking a boat leaving with a cargo of grain. Tucked in a corner were some barrels, very carefully wrapped up in rags to stop them being damaged in a storm and surrounded by more rubbish than you can imagine. It was the rubbish I noticed first because most boats are tidy places.

"'What's that?' I asked the Mate.

"'It's pitch,' he told me. "I never go out without some barrels of pitch on board for small repairs. There are boats at the bottom of the sea that would still be floating on top of it if they'd taken a barrel of pitch with them.'"

Mrs Moffat knew that the Mate had made a mistake. Trying to crack a joke with a customs officer was usually a sign that there was something going on.

Her husband continued. 'I told him that he'd wrapped his pitch up very comfortably for its voyage, and then suggested that it wasn't pitch at all. I was right. It was whisky, illegally brewed whisky. He was none too pleased when I had it taken ashore and he had to pay a hefty fine and leave without his precious pitch.'

Portsoy was the perfect place to be a child, the perfect place to have adventures and the perfect place to go exploring. Robert's older brothers must have kept a close eye on Robert as they hiked along the cliff-top path high above the small bay. Then there was the shore path, safe and dry at high tide and usually even safe at low tide. But in a storm! In a storm a man on a horse could have been washed away and never seen again. There were plenty of storms in Portsoy. There was also the busy harbour to explore. Boats came and went from all sorts of exciting places. Sailors spoke strange languages that Robert didn't understand.

Then there were the sounds of Portsoy, and Robert would remember them years later when he lived far away from Scotland. Gulls screeched to each other, sounding as though they were laughing at the fishermen from their rooftops. Chains rattled on the boats and a north-east wind blew the noise of their clanking much further than you would think. There was the slap of sails in the wind, especially wet sails, and the trundle of wheels as carts carried goods from the sailing boats up the very steep road from the harbour. Portsoy was small, busy and noisy – the ideal place to be a boy at the turn of the 18th century. Robert was born on 21st December 1795 and it was the years 1797 to 1806 that he spent in that wonderful village.

As there were no street lights, the Moffat boys and girls (there were eventually five boys and two girls in the family) did not go adventuring on dark winter nights. Instead they gathered in the customs officer's home around the open fire. There was a saying in those days that, 'the devil finds work for idle hands'. What that meant was that if people sat about wasting their time, the devil would tempt them to get up to mischief. There was not much time wasted in Robert's house. His mother had her hands full looking after her home and large family, but she still had time to teach them what she thought was important.

Those dark winter nights were spent round the fire with the children—boys as well as girls—learning to knit and sew. They darned their woollen socks and patched the holes in their clothes. As there was no spare money, nothing was thrown out that could be used again. It's a very funny thing, but people in the 21st century think that they invented recycling. Mrs Moffat, in the year 1800, could have taught us all a thing or two. A jacket worn by Robert's eldest brother would pass down to the next oldest, and then maybe to Robert himself. When it was too raggedy to be worn by anyone, the sleeves might be cut off and worn under long woollen socks to keep the biting winter wind from causing chilblains. The rest could be cut into patches to be used on other worn-out jackets. And the tiny bits and pieces left over would be knotted into a rag rug and laid before the fire for the children to sit on.

Children in Robert's day had a game they played. They sat on the rag rug, closed their eyes and pointed to a bit of the rug. Then whoever in the family could remember told the story of that rag and the others all chipped in with their memories. It might have gone something like this.

'I remember Granddad wearing that jacket. I didn't like it because it was so scratchy when he gave me a hug.'

'And I remember when Mother cut it down and made it into a coat for me.'

'I remember that I fell into the sea when I was wearing it. The jacket drank up so much water, and was so heavy, that it nearly dragged me under.'

'And I remember a patch from it on my breeches.'

'And I'm wearing the breeches,' the youngest might have said. 'And the patch is right here on my knee!'

Mrs Moffat didn't only teach her children to knit and sew she also taught them about God. Jesus was her Saviour and she loved him very much indeed. Her husband did too and both parents prayed for their children as well as teaching them the Bible. They knew that the Bible is the most important book in the whole world and they wanted Robert and his brothers and sisters to know that too.

The Moffat home was a poor one and there was no spare money to buy books. But among the few that they had were the Bible and the Shorter Catechism. The Shorter Catechism wasn't really very short – at least not to a boy like Robert. It's a book of questions and answers about the Bible and it was used to teach children. Of course, they had to learn to read before reading the Shorter Catechism for themselves. But, by the time Robert could read, he would have known many catechism questions and answers because children learned them by heart. Sunday afternoons in the Moffat home would often be spent answering catechism questions. In fact, it was from the first page of the Shorter Catechism that Robert learned the letters of the alphabet!

While Sundays were spent at church and learning about Jesus at home, Mondays to Saturdays were mostly spent outside. And, for Robert, that often meant going down to the harbour and trying to make himself useful to the sailors in the port. You might be wondering if he ever went to school. Yes, he did, but just for a very short time. There was no law in those days saying that boys and girls had to attend school, and many didn't. Robert went to the local school and was taught by a dominie (the Scottish word for a teacher in those days) whose name was Wullie Mitchell. Mr Mitchell was a stern man and not very patient with his pupils. Whether that had anything to do with Robert only staying a few weeks, nobody knows. Maybe it was more to do with the fact that the captain of one of the local boats liked Robert and sometimes took him out on his boat even as a young boy. Mr Wullie Mitchell probably didn't think much of that.

Robert was an adventurer at heart, and that must have given his mother and father a worry or two, especially when he decided to run away to sea. It's not clear when he did this, but it was certainly before he was eleven years old! Many years later he wrote, 'You would be surprised to hear how little I knew. I might have received a better education. My dear father and mother were not to blame, but I wanted to be a man before the time. I lived among shipping, and ran off to sea.'

The boy (remember he was younger than eleven!) set off to sea full of high hopes. 'No more school! No more lessons and no more being beaten by Wullie Mitchell's tawse!' A tawse was a leather strap used to punish school children. Their teacher smacked them across the hand with it and it was very sore.

For a while the young sailor's life was exciting, if very hard. Robert was expected to work like a man even though he was only a boy. His muscles ached and his hands bled and blistered.

'How can a tiny hack on your finger be so sore?' he asked himself, for the hundredth time, as salt sea water made his hand hurt until he nearly cried. There were even times when he was glad of the salt spray for it stopped anyone seeing his tears. It didn't take long for the boy to discover that a sailor's life was not for him and he couldn't wait for the boat to get back to his home in Portsoy.

'I got disgusted with a sailor's life,' Robert wrote, when he was an old man.

When he was eleven his father changed jobs. Mr Moffat was appointed to a job at Carronshore, which must have seemed very, very different to the children. Instead of living at a seaport with towering cliffs above it and the wild north-easterly wind blowing down from the Arctic Circle, their new home was a long way from the open sea. It was still a port, but a port on the River Carron that went into the River Forth not far to the north. And the Firth of Forth, at that point, is not much more than a mile wide.

How Robert must have missed the crashing waves, his jaunts along the coast with his friendly captain and the view from his favourite look-out spot on the cliffs. There was, however, exploring to be done in Carronshore and some hi-tech discoveries to be made.

'What's that strange boat?' Robert asked a new friend, as they found places to go and things to do.

'That's the famous *Charlotte Dundas*,' was the reply.

'She looks odd rather than famous,' commented Robert. 'What's her story?'

His friend knew it all. Everyone in Carronshore knew about the *Charlotte Dundas*.

'Well,' said the boy, 'coming from away up north you only know about sailing boats. But down here in the centre of things we know that the future is in paddle steamers not sailing ships.'

Robert was interested. This sounded good – though he might not quite have believed it.

'Can you see the paddle wheels on either side of the boat?' the boy asked.

Robert couldn't miss them. They reached from above deck level down into the sea.

'There's an engine in the hull powered by steam,' his friend continued. 'And when the steam gets up it works a crank that drives the paddle wheels.'

Robert was puzzled. 'What's the hull built of?' he asked. 'If it's wood there must be a danger of fire.'

The other boy shook his head. 'It is wood,' he admitted. 'But it's absolutely safe. You don't think the shipyard at Grangemouth would build a ship that was a fire hazard.'

By now the boys were right up beside the *Charlotte Dundas* and Robert felt he was looking at the boat of the future. Having developed an exploring mind in Portsoy, he now applied it to this amazing paddle steamer and wondered where in the world it could go.

'Could you cross the Atlantic Ocean in it?' he asked his friend.

'Don't be silly!' was the reply. 'You'd need to have so much coal on board to feed the engine that the vessel would sink. It's only built to work as a barge towing sloops up the River Forth.'

Robert's heart sank. He was an adventurer at heart not an inshore boatman!

It was while the Moffat family lived in Carronshore that Robert had his second experience of education, when he was sent with his older brother to Mr Paton's school. He was eleven years old at the time and his schooling only lasted six months. The subjects studied there were very different to what an eleven-year old would learn today. Robert was taught book-keeping (that's how to keep financial accounts) and mathematics. He was much more interested in astronomy, a subject that only the older boys were supposed to learn.

'How do you know about the Great Bear and Orion?' a friend asked him. 'You're not the right age for that class.'

Robert grinned. 'It's because we have such a long walk home from school. Father arranged with Mr Paton that I could stay behind and come home with my older brother. So I wait until the big boys are gathered round the teacher's table and then I creep up behind them and listen to what he's saying. If he's showing them anything interesting, I just push as far to the front as I can and spy on him without him seeing me.'

On dark winter nights he and his brother looked up to the stars and found the constellations they had heard about. Of course, in those days there was hardly any light pollution and the stars would have shone much more brightly than they do in towns and cities today.

It was by pushing forward through the older boys that Robert discovered that he liked geography too. He could never have enough. There was so much to learn about foreign places with strange names. The people there looked so different from Scottish people. They spoke languages hardly anyone understood. It was not only at school that the eleven-year-old heard about people from other parts of the world. Mrs Moffat learned about missionary work and told her children all she knew. Years after he left home he still remembered her reading a book to the family about missionaries working in Greenland and Labrador. It was exciting stuff!

A Very Early Start

'It can't be time to get up yet!' Robert growled. 'It's pitch dark.'

He turned over and pulled his blanket up over his head for it was cold. But that took the blanket away from his feet and his toes felt the cold too, which was just as well as it was time to get up and John Robertson, the head gardener, didn't think much of apprentices who weren't at their work on time.

Robert was now part of the workforce at Parkhill at Polmont. It wasn't far from his family but it was far enough. 'I wish I was in bed at Carronshore,' he muttered to himself under the blankets.

Knowing he had no choice, Robert hoisted himself out of bed, pulled on his breeches and staggered to the bowl of water that was waiting for him to wash his face. But he couldn't. The surface of the water, which had been sitting all night, had frozen. He cracked the ice with the side of his fist, cupped his hands, dipped them into the water and threw some on his face. If he wasn't properly awake before that, he certainly was after it.

An older apprentice shared his bothy (a small rough home where agricultural apprentices lived during their training).

'Will you get a move on!' the older boy said. 'It's four o'clock already.'

It was. But four o'clock on a winter's morning was not when a fourteen-year-old like Robert wanted to be up and working.

John Robertson was a good master. He didn't ask his apprentices to do what he wouldn't do himself. With spade in hand, he was ready and waiting for the boys when they appeared for work.

Robert shivered as he grabbed hold of his spade. His hands were so cold that he could hardly hold it.

'Knock your hands against the handle to heat them up,' Mr Robertson said, 'but not so hard as to break the skin. And do that every time the feeling goes from them,' he advised.

For two hours Robert dug along the line he was given.

'Put the blade of the spade in straight,' he was told, 'and heel it right down.'

Robert pushed his boot as hard as he could against the spade.

'Remember, the better the soil is prepared, the better the vegetables grow. And if they don't grow well, there'll be none for the Parkhill apprentices.'

So cold were Robert's hands that when the boys were told to stop for their bowl of porridge he didn't think he could open his fingers to let the spade go.

Mrs Robertson had the porridge ready in the kitchen when her husband and his apprentices eased off their boots and strode into the warmth of the range. (A range is an enclosed solid fuel cooker). Robert was desperate for heat and scared of it at the same time for he knew very well what would happen. As soon as the heat hit his hands the pain would start. When his fingers thawed from the tips downwards it was like a fire burning inside them and, until the burning stopped, he couldn't have held his porridge spoon if he'd been paid to.

The gardeners sat at the wooden table, each with a bowl of porridge in front of him and a smaller bowl of creamy milk beside it. There was no question of cooling down the porridge by pouring milk over it. That would have been a fearful waste of heat on a freezing cold morning. So lifting spoonfuls of boiling hot porridge they dipped them in the milk, taking just a tiny amount on to their horn spoons, and then put them in their mouths, letting the heat slide down and begin to warm them from the inside. When their breakfast was over and they had thawed through, it was time to go to work again – and the sun still hadn't risen!

'It's hard work at Parkhill,' Robert told his brothers and sisters, on his first visit home.

Mr Moffat heard the comment.

'Life's hard work, son,' he said. 'And it doesn't get any easier the older you grow.'

For three years, until 1812, Robert learned to labour like a man at Parkhill. He did well and at the end of his apprenticeship he went to work for the Earl of Moray at Donibristle. Once again he found himself near the sea in the County of Fife on the east coast of Scotland. It was just as well that Robert Moffat was used to working in the cold, for the wind that drives through Fife in the winter comes straight from the frozen plains of Siberia.

While life at Donibristle was hard work, there was time for fun too.

'Are you going to give us a tune on your fiddle?' Robert was asked on many an evening.

He never took much persuading.

'I've a new one for you tonight,' he told them. 'But it might still be a bit rusty for I've not done enough practising.'

With that he checked the tuning and began to play a Scots tune.

'What's that?' one of the apprentices asked.

'Can you not guess?'

Nobody could.

'It's something to do with where we are,' he hinted. 'And about the man who pays us.'

'I know!' laughed one of the apprentices, the one who had listened to his history lessons at school. 'Is it "The Bonnie Earl 'o Moray"?'

'It is indeed,' laughed Robert. 'And if you read the words of the ballad, you'll see that it's all about the killing of the Second Earl of Moray right here at Donibristle.'

Living near the sea, as they did, meant that swimming at Aberdour beach was a favourite sport in summer. And, as Robert was very athletic, he usually won the race to get there. On a day that was long remembered one of Robert's friends went out of his depth and got into real difficulties in the sea. Even in summer the water off the coast of Fife is very cold.

'Is he fooling around, do you think?' a boy asked.

Robert looked out to sea and realised there was no fooling in it. His friend was in trouble. With strong muscles built up through years of heavy work Robert powered through the water to where his companion was going under. Swimming behind him, he soon had his friend in his grip. Then, with one arm round him, Robert's strong legs took the strain of swimming back to the shore. Robert Moffat had saved a life.

A year later he was on the move again, this time to Cheshire in England.

While at Donibristle Robert had been able to visit his family from time to time, but they all knew that moving to Cheshire was different. In 1812 there was no easy way to travel that distance. His mother was aware of what a big step this was for her son so insisted on walking the first part of the way with him.

'Now Robert,' said Mrs Moffat, before she left him. 'I want to ask you a favour before we part. And I know you won't refuse to do what your mother wishes.'

'What is it?' asked Robert.

'Before I tell you, I want you to promise me that you'll do what I ask. Then I'll tell you what it is.'

Robert shook his head. 'I can't do that,' he said. 'I can't promise to do something before I know what it is.'

Mrs Moffat looked very sad. 'You know I love you. You don't think I'd ask you to promise to do something you couldn't do.'

The boy looked down at the ground to avoid his mother's eyes. She was silent so long that he couldn't bear it.

'Tell me what it is and I'll do it,' he said.

'I want you to promise to read a chapter of the Bible every morning and every evening.'

'But you know I read my Bible!' said the teenager.

His mother looked at him and he felt she was looking right into his heart.

'Yes, I know you read it, but not as often as you should. And I think you read it to please me rather than to please God. And read the Gospels,' said Mrs Moffat. 'Read the Gospels and pray and God will teach you.'

Having cornered her son into making that promise, Mrs Moffat kissed the sixteen-year-old, turned her back and walked towards home.

It took several days to travel to High Leigh in Cheshire where Robert was taking up a post as under-gardener. He arrived on Saturday, 26th December 1813 and was warmly welcomed.

'Tell us about your journey,' said one of the other gardeners, when they were getting to know each other.

'Well,' answered Robert, 'I walked to the coach that took me to Greenock, on the west coast of Scotland. That's where my boat left from. I don't know if there was a storm here, but we had a very rough voyage right into the teeth of a gale.'

His companion smiled. 'I imagine you did,' he agreed, 'for there was a fierce wind here too.'

'I was very glad when we were safely berthed in Liverpool and my legs were still shaky when I came off the boat!' Robert told him. 'Then I took a coach from Liverpool and I was right glad to arrive. It seemed a long six days.'

'So you're a real land-lubber then!' laughed the other gardener.

Robert shook his head. 'I am not!' he said. 'In fact, I was at sea before I ever took up gardening!'

Mr and Mrs Leigh of High Leigh were good employers and kind too. The head gardener knew a fine worker when he saw one, and in a couple of years Robert was given much more important jobs to do than most of the other 18-year-olds who worked there.

'This is a good place to be,' he wrote home. 'It's hard work but my boss is fair and tells us when we've done well rather than just giving us a row when we've done something wrong. And Mrs Leigh seems to like me. She was surprised to learn that I like reading and she's lent me some of her books. I make quite sure that my hands are clean before I touch them,' he added, thinking that's exactly what his mother would tell him to do.

It was just at this exciting and interesting time of his life that two things happened to unsettle Robert and set him thinking.

'Would you like to come to one of our meetings?' a friendly neighbour asked.

Robert wasn't sure. The neighbour went to the Methodist church and at that time not everyone approved of it. The young man decided to go and found that it was different from any church he'd been at before. The service upset Robert. He had gone thinking he was a Christian, and he left it thinking he wasn't.

Sometime later he wrote about that difficult experience.

'For many weeks I was miserable. I tried to feel I was a Christian, but I couldn't. Then I thought that I could become as bad as I could possibly be and then, if I became a Christian, my life would be so different that I'd know for sure I was saved. I read my Bible and I prayed. Because I lived on my own in the lodge house I could spend all my spare time thinking and reading.'

And it was as he was reading his Bible alone in the lodge that he knew for sure that Jesus had died to save him from his sins and that he, Robert Moffat, would go to heaven when he died. Soon afterwards the young man wrote to his parents to tell them that he had been converted and that he was going to become a

Methodist. While his father and mother were very, very happy that their son had become a Christian, they were just a little worried about him changing churches. Mr and Mrs Leigh didn't like it either and she even stopped lending him books to read.

You see, joining the Methodist church was frowned on by many in the Church of England in those days. Some people didn't like the 'enthusiasm' of the Methodists… it wasn't dignified in their opinion. The Methodists were too 'emotional'. Some people just didn't like the fact that people were going to a different church. They felt that everyone should go to the established church… the official one. But more and more people went to other churches and chapels to hear God's Word being preached simply because many of the traditional, official churches were no longer preaching the truth of the Bible and were no longer being blessed with the power of God. That's why Robert Moffat and others like him went to the Methodists.

This new church was the first big thing that happened to Robert after moving south to Cheshire. The next big thing was that the young man found a poster for a meeting that was already over.

It happened like this. One day Robert decided to visit Warrington, a town about six miles from High Leigh. It was a lovely summer evening and he enjoyed the walk. As he crossed over a bridge at the entrance to the town he noticed a poster. The young man was in no hurry at all and stopped to read what it said. It was advertising a meeting run by the London Missionary Society and it said that a minister, Rev William Roby of Manchester, would be taking the meeting. Robert had never heard of the London Missionary Society and he certainly had never heard of Rev William Roby.

After reading the poster several times, the teenager noticed that the meeting was past. His shoulders sagged and, instead of spending much time in Warrington, he did just what he had to do and then turned round and walked the six miles home. As he did so the words on the poster went round and round in his mind. The word 'missionary' especially struck him and he remembered the missionary stories his mother had told him and his brothers and sisters when they were all children together back home in Scotland. There are times when something worms its way into your head and just won't go away. That's exactly what happened to Robert Moffat as he crossed the bridge into Warrington.

All Change!

'I could never be a missionary,' the young man thought, as he strode home to High Leigh. 'I've only been to school for a few months in all my life!'

Along the road he went, looking at the fields and hedges but not really seeing them. His mind was so far away.

'I couldn't go to college or university,' he told himself. 'The London Missionary Society, whoever they are, will want clever people who've done a lot of studying. They won't want the likes of me.'

Reaching a crossroads, he checked he was going in the right direction and walked on.

'When I was a boy all I wanted to do was be a sailor,' Robert remembered. 'Now I just want to be a gardener, a really good gardener. I want to grow good vegetables and fruits, even some of the new exotic fruits that are coming into Britain. I want to find out how to grow them well and then teach the new apprentices how it's done.'

As he walked, Robert knew in his heart that he wasn't telling himself the truth. What had been true as he walked towards Warrington quite simply wasn't true on the way back. What he really wanted to do was be a missionary.

By the time he was back in his lodge house Robert had decided that, even though the missionary meeting was over, he would go and see Rev William Roby, the man whose name was on the poster. His home was in Manchester and as soon as he was able to get there, Robert found himself walking along the road towards Mr Roby's door.

'This is it,' he said, stopping outside the house.

Robert's courage failed him and he turned away. Anyone watching from the house across the road would have wondered what was happening. A young man walked backwards and forwards along the street, sometimes stopping outside a house and almost climbing up the steps to the door ... before turning away and walking up the street again. Years later Robert himself explained what happened.

'At last, after walking backward and forward for a few minutes, I returned to the door and knocked. This was no sooner done than I would have given a thousand pounds, if I had possessed them, not to have knocked; and I hoped, how I hoped with all my heart, that Mr Roby might not be at home ...'

Mr Roby was at home and Robert was invited in to speak to him. They had a long talk and the young man told his whole story, even explaining about how little time he had been at school.

When all their talking was done Mr Roby sat back in his chair.

'I'll write to the London Missionary Society,' he said. 'And I'll tell them exactly what you've told me.'

He did just that and not long afterwards had a reply saying that they didn't think Robert was suitable for mission work. But Mr Roby had seen the young man and was quite sure they were wrong. The minister wrote again ... and again, until eventually the Directors of the Mission agreed to begin training Robert to be a missionary. Yet again Mr Roby sat down at his desk to write a letter, this time to Robert to tell him the news and to suggest that he should try to get a job near Manchester. That would allow him to spend time studying with Mr Roby himself.

'I think you are making a very big mistake,' Mrs Leigh said, some weeks later, when Robert went to his employers to tell them that he was leaving. 'When you first came here I thought you were a fine young man. But since you went to the Methodists you've become far too keen about Christianity. You should settle down and be a good gardener. That's what you should do.'

Thinking back to how kind she had been when he first arrived, Robert felt sad that Mrs Leigh felt as she did. But he knew that he had to do what God wanted him to do rather than what she wanted. Having said goodbye, he took up his bag full of all that belonged to him in the world, and headed for Manchester. The following week Robert sat down and wrote to his parents.

'I am now well settled at Dukinfield, a fine nursery garden run by Mr Smith. He's a good boss and he has agreed to have me work for him most days each week and spend the other days studying with Mr Roby, who is a friend of his. I have so much to learn! The Smiths are kind to me. They have four children. The oldest, Mary, is a few months older than I am and the others are all younger boys. Mr Smith is Scottish and he, like me, came down to England to work. Mrs Smith is English. Mary is a fine girl and very interested in mission work. She couldn't ever be anything else for her parents talk about missions all the time. Well, that's not quite true of Mr Smith, because he's a splendid nursery gardener and he talks a lot about plants too.'

Meanwhile Mr Roby was in touch with the London Missionary Society.

'Robert Moffat is now settled with the Smiths at Dukinfield. With him working so close by I'll be able to observe the kind of man he is and whether he is really suitable for mission work. He is certainly very keen to study but he has so much to learn.'

Robert agreed with him there. He really did have a great deal to learn. Right from the beginning, Robert Moffat worked hard both in the market garden and in his studies. To his surprise he discovered that he enjoyed studying.

At the beginning of September 1816, Robert looked around the garden at Dukinfield. Vegetables were being harvested and the apples and pears were swelling on the branches.

'You'll be away before they're ready,' one of the apprentices said, for Robert was leaving … to be a missionary in Africa!

'So I will,' his friend agreed. 'But there's so much to do I'm not sure where to start.'

The apprentice grinned. 'If I were you, I'd start by going for the coach or you'll not see your family before you leave the country.'

Robert Moffat laughed. 'You're right … and I'm off.'

A few days later he was back home in Scotland with his father and mother, brothers and sisters. Several of them were away from home working, but they'd come back to say goodbye to the family adventurer. While they were all happy to see each other there was still sadness in the air. So many missionaries who went to Africa never returned.

Back down in Dukinfield someone else was thinking along exactly the same lines.

'We love each other,' Mary Smith told her father. 'And Robert has lived here with us so long that you know what a good man he is.'

Mr and Mrs Smith sat together and looked at their eldest child, their only daughter.

'Robert is a good man,' said her father. 'There's no question about that. And if he'd been staying here in England, we would have been happy for you to marry.'

Mrs Smith agreed. 'You know Robert's like a son to us now,' she told her daughter. 'And it's hard to see him go where he might be eaten by lions or murdered by savages.'

Her husband was less dramatic but just as firm. 'I've heard of so many men who've become missionaries only to die of fever within months of arriving. And what's even sadder, some of them had young wives with them who only lived a few weeks in the terrible conditions they had to face.'

Mary loved Robert very much. She was also a missionary at heart. Yet she couldn't defy her parents and go against their will. Apart for hurting them, the London Missionary Society would not have allowed her to go when her mother and father felt so strongly against it.

Mr and Mrs Smith were not unreasonable people and they allowed Mary to go to London to Robert's farewell service. It was 30th September and a crowd of people gathered in Surrey Chapel to say goodbye to eight young men. Four were going to the South Seas and four, including Robert, were going to Africa.

Handing each of the men a Bible, the minister who took the service spoke to them all very seriously. Then the eight young men promised to live as the Bible teaches, and to tell others about the Lord Jesus.

Three weeks later Robert climbed aboard the sailing ship *Alacrity*. There was plenty of time to think over the weeks and months that followed, for the voyage took eighty-six days! No doubt Robert thought a great deal about Mary. Perhaps he also thought back to his childhood in Carronshore and wondered if the *Charlotte Dundas* was still paddling along the Firth of Forth with steam belching out its funnel. Looking up he saw the sails above him, filled with wind that would take them to Africa. 'I'm glad I'm sailing to Africa. I don't think those steam pistons in wooden-hulled boats will ever catch on. They are just far too dangerous. Sailing really is the only way to travel.'

It was on the 13th January 1817 that Robert Moffat first stood on African soil. The *Alacrity* berthed at Cape Town and that was his introduction to the great continent.

'Look at the fort,' said the man who met him off the boat. 'That was built by the East India Company. They run everything here, including you and me.'

'It's a curious shape,' commented Robert, studying the great hulk of a building.

'That's because it's built in the shape of a star, the star being the crest of the East Indian Company.'

'What do you mean, that they 'run you and me'?' the Scot asked.

His new friend smiled.

'Well,' he was told, 'it's like this. We have to do what the Governor says. And the East India Company is so powerful in South Africa that what the Governor says and what the East India Company says is most often the same thing. For example, if your work takes you over the borders of the Colony, you need the Governor's permission to go. And if, for any reason, the East India Company thinks that you being there could risk spoiling their trade, you won't get permission to go.'

'It sounds very complicated,' Robert said. 'But I'm sure we'll get permission to go to wherever God wants us to be.'

Walking through the streets of Cape Town was a very strange experience for Robert Moffat.

'The houses are all just one storey high,' he commented.

'That keeps them cooler in summer,' he was told. 'It gets really hot here.'

'And they look so clean with nearly all of them painted white.'

His companion laughed. 'Same thing,' he said. 'White paint reflects the sun and helps keep the inside of the houses cool.'

Having been a gardener, Robert couldn't help but notice the amazing colours of the plants and flowers that were growing all around them. He would happily have stopped and explored them, but the man at his side was walking more quickly than the new missionary's sea-legs wanted to go. After eighty-six days on the *Alacrity*, Robert was ready for a seat that didn't rock slowly side to side.

Keen to know what his work was going to be, Robert was pleased to learn the Mission's plans for him very soon after he arrived.

'We want you to work in the kraal of a chief who lives beyond the Orange River in Namaqualand,' he was told.

'Does that mean I need the Governor's permission to go there?' Robert asked.

'Yes, it does, and that might take some time,' the senior missionary answered. 'But let me tell you more. The chief is called Africaner and he's interesting and unpredictable. There are many wild stories told about him and probably not all of them are true. He's certainly an outlaw with a price on his head and probably a murderer too. But there are stories about him welcoming missionaries, though he can change from being a friend to a threat very quickly. You're starting your missionary life with a big challenge, but I'm sure you'll meet bigger ones still in the years to come.'

Robert tried to take in what he was being told. 'I suppose if Chief Africaner is an outlaw the Governor will want me to go there to see if I can help.'

'We'll just have to wait and see,' he was told. 'We've already applied for permission.'

The Governor refused permission for Robert to travel to Namaqualand.

'Why?' Robert asked when he heard the news.

The senior missionary opened the letter.

'The Governor says that escaped servants and slaves have gone over the Colony borders into Namaqualand and that missionaries who've been there in the past have only asked them to go back home rather than forcing them to go.'

Robert didn't understand.

'That means that those who escaped can't be punished because the Governor has no powers over the border.'

It took months for the Governor to change his mind and issue permission for Robert to travel. But the new young missionary didn't waste that time. He learned the Dutch language, became a good horseman and he also learned many practical things that would be of use to him later. For example, as he knew he was going to travel in a covered wagon pulled by oxen, he studied how to handle oxen and how to keep a covered wagon in good repair. And when his socks wore into holes and his clothes were torn, Robert remembered his childhood home and was grateful to his mother for teaching him to knit and sew.

As the young man waited for his travel permit to come he often thought of Mary. He wished she was with him as he prepared to go to Namaqualand, but the thought of working with an outlaw and a murderer told him that Mr Smith was quite right to keep her at home, at least for the time being.

On the Move

It wasn't until September that Robert and two other missionaries, Mr and Mrs Kitchingman, were given permission to leave the Colony and head for the land beyond the Orange River and the kraal of the infamous Africaner. Getting permission was one thing, getting there was quite another. And planning was a huge job. Things kept rumbling around Robert's head and he had to remember to write them all down.

'I've never had to pack animals before,' he thought, 'but if I don't take beasts with me I won't be able to breed them for food when I get to Namaqualand. They'll provide fertiliser too for growing vegetables, which reminds me I need to take vegetable seeds.' His mind wouldn't stop buzzing. 'Then I'll need a spade and hoe.' The list just went on and on … and on and on … and every single thing had to be carried at a walking pace for months.

'The journey from Carronshore to High Leigh was absolutely nothing compared to this,' the young man smiled. 'And I thought it was a six-day adventure. Our next adventure will take months and travelling will be very much rougher than the sea ever was between Greenock and Liverpool.'

Mr and Mrs Kitchingman agreed. They were travelling with Robert as far as Bysondermeid and after that he would be on his own with the African wagon driver and all the porters. Now that permission was granted, the days were full of arrangements. Not for them train tickets, aircraft boarding passes and satellite navigation. Their travels were altogether different.

'So this is my home for the next few months,' Robert thought, looking at the covered wagon which was to be drawn by sixteen or eighteen oxen. 'These are all my worldly possessions,' he exclaimed, packing boxes into the wagon. 'And these are your fellow travellers,' commented a friend, who was helping him to prepare.

Robert looked at the large group of porters. He'd heard stories about porters abandoning people miles from anywhere and leaving them to be attacked by wild animals. His porters didn't look particularly friendly or especially pleased to be going.

'This isn't too bad a start,' Robert said, when the wheels of his wagon began to roll.

Mrs Kitchingman agreed, for the road was smooth at first. Before many hours had passed, however, it was no more than a track.

'It's like being on a ship in a storm,' she told her husband. 'The wagon rocks and rolls from side to side.'

Mr Kitchingman nodded and wondered how his wife would feel when the track ran out and they were on rough ground.

The oxen that seemed to know the direction when they started became more than a little stubborn towards the end of each day.

'We move so slowly,' Robert said to himself. 'I'll be an old man with a long white beard by the time we get there!'

A few hours later Robert smiled when he remembered his thought about a long white beard because he suddenly realised that nothing that had started white was white any longer. The dust of Africa settled everywhere as they lumbered on and things lost their colour underneath it. They were entering a sand-coloured world.

'The mealies are doing well,' he commented, as the long train of oxen trudged between fields almost ripe for harvest.

Mrs Kitchingman looked around her. 'They need to do well for that's the people's main food.'

Thinking back to the apples and pears swelling on the branches at Dukinfield, Robert compared them with the peaches and apricots that grew in South Africa.

'We thought we had great peaches in the glasshouses at home,' said he. 'But they are nothing compared with these ones!'

As the days wore on, they trundled further and further from the city, but still in farmed land. Sheep grazed the rougher land and from time to time they came across oxen, especially as they neared homesteads.

Two weeks later they were still on the move, lumbering through poorer land now. Another difference was that the homesteads were further apart, days apart, and they were smaller too. On and on they went, going slowly and steadily for they had to spare the oxen, not knowing how long they'd be on the trail together, nor always certain of either fodder or water.

The journey was never boring. Robert had seen wild animals in Scotland and England, but not the kind of wild animals he was seeing now.

'I just love the springboks!' he said to Mrs Kitchingman. 'They look as if they have springs in their legs.' Then he laughed aloud and his horse turned round and looked at him. 'Of course! That's why they're called springboks!'

'I'd not thought of that either,' laughed Mrs Kitchingman.

She didn't laugh as often now for the journey was really tough going. Everything was dirty, everyone was dirty, and it was taking her time to get used to that.

The springboks could do a curious thing. They could be standing stock-still and then suddenly be in the air and turn in the other direction. Not for them a run and then a jump. They were expert at a standing start to mid-air technique and it impressed the young missionary. One did that just a few feet away and then another joined the fun. Mrs Kitchingman laughed at their antics and both her husband and Robert felt the better of her laughter.

While the journey was never boring it was never comfortable either. The porters' hobby seemed to be arguing amongst themselves, arguments that broke into fights too quickly.

'If there's something worse than hearing people arguing in your own language it's hearing them arguing when you don't know what they're saying!' Robert decided. 'It could be about nothing at all or about leaving us stranded and we'd never know!'

Suddenly everything ground to a halt and voices were raised behind him. He went to investigate. Several porters were on their knees beside a wagon and their arms were waving in all directions. It took Robert a few minutes to realise that a wagon wheel was the problem. It was slipping on its axle and in danger of falling off.

'I'm glad we had those months before leaving,' the young man said.

Mr Kitchingman agreed. 'It gave us time to learn a thing or two about wagon wheels!'

It took a long time, for nothing happened quickly in the searing heat, but at last the thing was mended and they were ready to get on their way again. But the oxen were not. There was a rebellion in the ranks! Having stopped for a repair, they decided they were stopped for the day and it took a great deal of effort to get them to think otherwise.

'I think there's a homestead in the far distance,' Robert said, when he noticed that the grazing land was changing to crops. Some miles along the track he saw black men and women working on the land. Travelling by wagon meant that they were seen long before arriving at the lonely homestead.

'The Boers have come a long way from home over the years,' said the Scotsman. 'I wonder how many greats their grandfathers had when they sailed from the Netherlands to Africa.'

Mrs Kitchingman did some counting in her head. 'I think it could have been as much as their great, great, great, great, great, great, great, great grandfathers.'

'Well done!' her husband laughed. 'You're good at arithmetic!'

'It seems sad,' Robert thought aloud, 'that the farms are all owned by Boers, who are white Dutch-speakers, and the local black Africans, the Hottentots, are their servants and slaves. I suppose that helps us though. The Hottentots who work for Boers have had to learn Dutch to do their jobs which means that we can speak to them all about Jesus for they understand the same language.'

That's why Robert Moffat learned Dutch in his months in Cape Town rather than one of the African languages.

It took a very long time from seeing the homestead in the distance to actually reaching it and the farmer walked a good way out to meet them.

'Welcome, friends,' he shouted, when they neared each other. 'You're the first white people I've seen in the last three months!'

Robert introduced them and explained that they were missionaries.

'Mynheer Moffat, you are welcome to our home, and doubly welcome for being a missionary,' said the farmer. He led them to his house leaving the Hottentots to look after the porters and the animals.

The missionaries were treated as very special guests. They were special guests, for visitors came months apart to these faraway homesteads!

'We can have a proper service tonight,' the farmer told his family, 'and not just the usual reading from the Bible and prayer.'

Many Boers at that time would have a Bible reading and prayer together each evening, and some would have the same each morning too.

Having been travelling for so long Robert and the Kitchingmans had become used to the simplest of food and not very much of it.

'That's wonderful,' Mrs Kitchingman said when the meal was laid out.

'We grow all our own food,' the farmer's wife explained. 'Of course, that means that it's fresher than you could ever buy in a market anywhere.'

Robert told them that he had been a gardener and so knew the taste of the freshest of fresh vegetables and fruit. But none had ever tasted so good before and the farmer's wife was right pleased to hear that! He had forgotten how sweet mutton was and the milk ran over his throat like honey.

When the meal was finished, the farmer brought out a big Bible and all his family gathered for a service.

Robert looked around the room. 'Where are the servants?' he asked.

'Servants!' gasped the farmer. 'What do you mean "the servants"?'

'I mean the Hottentots,' the missionary said. 'I've seen them working on the farm and in your home.'

The man was confused, and sometimes when people are confused they say more than they should. That's exactly what happened in that lonely farmhouse.

'The Hottentots! Is that what you mean?' he stormed. 'Let me go to the mountains and call the baboons. I'll give you a congregation of baboons if you like.'

Then he looked at his sons who were gathered around for the service.

'No,' he said to them. 'You go and call the dogs from the door. They'll do for a congregation.'

Robert made no comment on what had been said. Instead he led the family in singing praise to God and in reading the Bible. He chose his reading carefully.

'Leaving that place, Jesus withdrew to the region of Tyre and Sidon. A Canaanite woman from that vicinity came to him, crying out, "Lord, Son of David, have mercy on me! My daughter is suffering terribly from demon-possession."

Jesus did not answer a word. So his disciples came to him and urged him, "Send her away, for she keeps crying out after us."

He answered, "I was sent only to the lost sheep of Israel."

The woman came and knelt before him. "Lord, help me," she said.

He replied, "It is not right to take the children's bread and toss it to their dogs."

"Yes, Lord," she said, "but even the dogs eat the crumbs that fall from the master's table."

Then Jesus answered, "Woman, you have great faith. Your request is granted."

And her daughter was healed from that very hour.' (Matthew 15:21-28)

The farmer frowned as Robert began to speak. He had just said that the dogs could come to the service rather than the Hottentots, and here was Jesus saying that someone who, like a dog, could get crumbs of good things from him had great faith!

Although Robert was speaking, the farmer had no choice but interrupt him.

'Will Mynheer sit down and wait a little,' he said. 'He shall have the Hottentots.'

The man's sons, who had been told to bring in the dogs, went and brought the Hottentots instead and they all gathered together, white people and black people. So Boers and Hottentots worshipped God together. Later, after the Hottentots had left the house, the farmer turned to Robert, 'My friend, you took a hard hammer and you have broken a hard head.'

* * *

When the wagon train left the homestead the missionaries began their trundling way up hills that led to mountains that would eventually take them to Namaqualand. As they trekked, he thought about the people of the land.

'What a history the Hottentots have had,' he said to his friends. 'They were the people who lived here originally. Then around AD 1500 explorers and tradesmen came from Europe bringing many good things, but also carrying smallpox with them. It was such a terrible disease that nearly half of the local people died of the pox in just a few years.'

Robert's thoughts were interrupted by a colossal snort from an ox that was furious at having stood on an anthill. Porters, clawing at the sandy track to free the beast's foreleg, were not best pleased either. The ants were scampering up their arms in thousands, much quicker than they could brush them off. It was over an hour before they started on their way again and tempers were not good as it was so hot.

When all had settled down a bit, Robert went back to his history.

'It was another hundred years till the Dutch East India Company set up a shipping station at the Cape of Good Hope. And that was the beginning of the end of the Hottentots' traditional way of life. They had lived on the land and now their lands were taken away from them. The incomers from the Netherlands divided it into fields and took it as their own. The African people were pushed further and further from their traditional homelands. Having nowhere to grow crops, nowhere to graze their animals, they had no choice but to become servants and slaves.'

Mr Kitchingman shook his head sadly. 'They even lost their name,' he said. 'The word Hottentot was not their original name; it was just a rough effort at copying a traditional African word.' Then a thought crossed his mind. 'I suppose the Boers lost their name too as the word Boer is "trekboeren" shortened and "trekboeren" just means "wandering farmers".'

Robert got up to look at yet another broken wagon wheel before muttering to himself, 'So one set of wandering farmers pushed another set of wandering farmers off their land. Sad.'

Burning Hoofs

Many weeks later the wagon train reached Bysondermeid. This was where Robert Moffat and his friends were to part. By then they were all utterly exhausted, as were the porters. Even the oxen were worn down and couldn't have carried on much longer. For a month they all stayed there recovering from the trek. Then, having said goodbye to Mr and Mrs Kitchingman, and with only his wagon train driver and the porters as companions, Robert faced his hardest challenges yet.

Even beyond Bysondermeid they came on the occasional homestead, but what he heard from the farmers didn't always cheer him up.

'You're going to work with Africaner!' one exclaimed. 'He killed my two brothers and he'll kill you too. He'll set you up as a target for his boys to practice their shooting.'

Another farmer – one with a very vivid imagination – had another suggestion. 'You know the talking drums?' he asked Robert. The missionary said that he did. 'Well, Africaner will kill you and skin you and use your skin to cover his drum. And the first message he'll send on his new talking drum will be that he's just killed the missionary.'

'Do you have a mother at home in Scotland?' asked the farmer's wife.

'Yes,' replied Robert, 'and a father, brothers and sisters as well.'

The woman wiped a tear from her eye.

'Is there a girl at home that you love?' she went on.

This woman was not scared of asking personal questions! Perhaps that was because she saw so few people out in the wilds as she was.

Robert thought of Mary. 'Yes, I do,' he told her.

That evening, as they talked, the missionary remembered all that he'd left behind and told the good woman about Mary, Dukinfield and Mr Roby. Then it was the woman's turn to talk and her only subject was the infamous Africaner.

The next day, when the oxen were up and ready to go, the woman wiped away her tears.

'Had you been an old man,' she said, 'it would have been nothing, for you would soon have died anyway. But you are young, too young to be killed by that monster Africaner.'

What a way to say goodbye!

Another Boer farmer whose homestead Robert visited in his long months of trekking suggested that Africaner would have a good use for Robert's skull – he would have it made into a drinking cup!

Eventually the rough track that the missionary and his companions were following ceased to exist and sand surrounded them on every side. Mile after mile they lumbered on, the sand getting ever deeper as they went. It grew higher too, for the desert wasn't flat. Hills and mountains marked their way, all sand and none of it stable. A sudden wind would change the contour of a hill or engulf the oxen's legs up to their thighs. Oxen are enormously strong creatures but they can't pull their legs out of sand that deep.

Robert looked around. There was nothing green to be seen, no trees, no bushes, not a single blade of grass. He had been travelling long enough to know that the journey was about to become dangerously hard. If there was nothing green, it was because there was no water and no water meant .... He didn't want to think what it meant. Robert Moffat prayed about this and he prayed hard. He knew that his companions all understood much better than he did what would happen if they couldn't find water. They didn't want to die of thirst and he knew they were in danger of deserting.

Rather than travelling during the heat of the day the oxen pulled the wagon in the dark and cooler night hours. The animals hauled with all their might, but there were still times when they couldn't make the wagon budge, so deep was it embedded in the sand. One night, when they should have been starting to trek, the oxen wouldn't or couldn't stand up. Even after a day resting they were exhausted and nearly desperate with thirst.

'We'll not try to move them until the coolest time of night,' Robert said to his ox driver. 'And we'll pray that we'll find water before they die.'

It was the hot season of the year and even though it was dark the sand was still roasting. As the men lay down, the warm air had them pouring with perspiration and the hot sand beneath them then drained it into the ground. The oxen's breathing was shallow and Robert knew they were in real danger. In the early hours of the morning the men were awake with raging thirst. Harnessing the oxen to the wagon was useless. They were totally incapable of moving themselves let alone hauling the weight of the wagon behind them, even if the men had the strength to dig the wheels free of sand – which they didn't.

'We need to find water,' said Robert. 'We'll leave the wagon here with some of the porters and find the most likely place to dig for a spring.'

The men did not look convinced that this was a good idea.

'But we'll have to take the oxen with us so that they can drink any water we find. We can't carry it back to them.'

So Robert and some of the porters encouraged, cajoled and forced the poor parched creatures to their feet and led them to a hollow in a sandy mountain. Then, despite being totally exhausted themselves, the men dug and dug until they reached damp sand. Then they dug deeper until the tiniest trickle of water appeared. Oxen can smell water and they were scratching at the sand with their hoofs in sheer desperation.

'Drink a little,' the missionary told his porters. 'You'll be ill if you take too much too soon.'

But there was no question of them taking too much as there was so little there.

As his companions licked the water from their hands, Robert looked at it and remembered his sailing days.

'This is just like bilge water from a ship,' he thought, for it was nearly black and sandy and not very good at all. But it was water!

When the men had drunk enough to keep themselves digging, they started once again. Men less expert in living in the desert might have drunk more water themselves rather than thinking of their oxen. But the porters knew that if the oxen died, they wouldn't survive themselves. So they set about digging deeper and deeper to find water for the beasts. Like the men, the animals could only safely drink a little at first or they would have been ill.

Hours were spent that night digging in hot sand. When the oxen were taken to drink their hoofs made the sand slide down into the hole and covered the water.

'Keep digging round about them,' the ox driver said. 'Don't stop or the sand will avalanche in and we'll be smothered.'

That's how deep they had to dig!

By the time the last of the oxen had some water, the first of them was ready for a second drink of the filthy stuff. So the night passed and Robert and his men were utterly exhausted though the oxen were a little refreshed.

A new danger awaited them as they left the water hole.

'What's wrong with that one?' he asked, when one of the beasts seemed skittish as they trekked back to the wagon.

Then another was the same, and another.

The problem was that the sun was reaching its height and the sand had become so hot that it was burning the oxen's hoofs. They were almost dancing in desperation as they tried to keep their hoofs from being cooked! Near the wagon was a slight hollow where the sand wasn't quite so deep. Robert and his companions herded the oxen into the hollow and kept them together. That created shadow and stopped the sun beating down on their feet.

God has made creatures so amazingly well that they instinctively try to save their lives when in terrible danger. That's what these oxen did. They pressed together to keep their feet in the shade of their own bodies. Those in full sun on the outside pushed towards the centre and the shade of the others. If you'd been watching from above, you would have seen a herd of oxen crammed together but constantly moving from the outside in and from the inside out. While Robert's men were struggling to keep themselves alive and to save the oxen, the thought of Africaner and the danger he posed was the least of his troubles.

Later, Robert wrote of another time on that long journey when he and his men were saved from near starvation. On this occasion their oxen made a bid for freedom and lumbered away while the men were asleep. The porters went off in search of them while Robert and the wagon driver stayed behind. Food supplies were dangerously low.

'For three days I remained with my wagon driver on this burning plain, with scarcely a breath of wind, and what there was felt as if it was coming from the mouth of an oven. We had only tufts of dry grass to make a small fire, or rather a flame. And little fire was needed because we had hardly any food to prepare. We saw no human being, not a single antelope or beast of prey made its appearance. But in the dead of the night we sometimes heard the roar of a lion on the mountain. At last, some men arrived on horseback, two of them having mutton tied to their saddles.'

Robert, who was nearly starving, finished his account by saying, 'I can't imagine anyone looking at a table absolutely covered with wonderful food with half the delight I looked at that mutton!'

No wonder the mutton tasted so good, for apart from animals that they'd killed for food, the nearest Robert got to eating meat was chewing biltong. Sometimes as he chewed it he smiled and remembered the day he first met the stuff. It was at a homestead right at the beginning of his trek and a farmer had held out a strip of biltong to him.

'No, thank you,' said Robert, 'I don't chew tobacco.'

At that time some people chewed tobacco as some children chew gum today. Others smoked tobacco, but neither chewing it nor smoking it did them good.

However, this wasn't tobacco. The farmer laughed aloud.

'What a lot you have to learn!' he said. 'When you kill an animal you don't eat all the meat at once. You cut some of it into strips and hang them out in the sun to dry.'

The missionary realised that it was so hot that it would dry very quickly and, once dried, it would keep well and not rot.

'When you are on your trek,' the farmer told him, 'biltong keeps you chewing and that makes you feel full even if you're not. And it makes the water run in your mouth when there's nothing to drink. It takes a long time to chew through a strip of biltong. It's great stuff!'

Robert had discovered that to be true but, good though biltong was, it was not a hundredth as delicious as the mutton those men brought on their horses that day.

What was even better than the mutton was that one of the horsemen was Mr Bartlett, another missionary! He was on his way to Pella and had met Robert's porters while they were looking for their runaway animals.

'Your men are bringing fresh oxen,' he told Robert. 'They're coming more slowly so as not to tire them out.'

The young missionary thought that was the best news he could hear, but there was better to come.

'You're not far from Pella!' said Mr Bartlett. 'A few more days and you'll be there. Then, after you and your men are well rested, you can cross the Orange River.'

'And so to Africaner,' added Robert, thinking of all the stories he'd heard about the outlaw.

Mr Bartlett nodded.

'And so to Africaner,' he agreed.

The porters arrived with fresh oxen that were more used to deep sand. Dragging the wagon was less of a problem for them. Mr Bartlett stayed with Robert and his men until the wagon was ready to roll and then travelled with them to Pella where his wife was waiting to welcome the new young missionary.

I'd almost forgotten what it was like not to live in a wagon,' Robert told Mrs Bartlett. 'And to eat at a table too,' he laughed.

There was a mirror in the house at Pella and Robert had quite a shock when he saw himself in it. Having started the trek as a muscular young man, his face now looked thin and old.

'Will I ever get rid of the sand from my hair,' he wondered.

The answer was probably not.

His muscles had tightened and were now wiry and hard. They would need to be for he had heavy work still to come. That night he lay in a bed for the first time in months and thought about Mary.

Namaqualand at Last!

Robert Moffat and his fellow travellers had seen little enough water for months and now they were standing at the side of the Orange River with water enough for any number of men and animals.

'What a wonderful sight!' said the young missionary to the African teacher, who had come to take him from Pella over the river to Africaner's kraal.

Then he looked at the wagon, the oxen, the men and all they'd brought with them, and thought how interesting it was going to be getting them all to the other side of the Orange River. The gardener in him immediately remembered his precious seeds. Whatever was soaked in the crossing, the seeds had to be kept dry or they would sprout before they were planted.

'Pull the rope tighter,' one of the porters yelled, as he held willow logs side by side with the weight of his body while they were lashed together to make a raft.

Another log was added and then another until the porters decided that the raft was big enough to begin its job. Meanwhile everything had been unpacked from the wagon.

'Take off its cover now,' Robert told one of his men. 'And then dismantle it.'

The cover was the colour of desert sand. Two men climbed up on to the sides of the wagon and removed it, folded the fabric and laid it on top of one of the boxes. Robert watched as his travelling home was taken to pieces and laid at the riverside.

'Are you ready for the first lot to go over?' asked the teacher, looking round at the piles that had to go from one side to the other.

'We're ready,' he was told. 'What's first?'

The porters decided that, if they took the pieces of the wagon across first and then fitted it together again, they could put the things they'd taken out of it right back where they belonged as they were rafted over. For two whole days they worked, going backwards and forwards over the river, only stopping in the hottest part of the day for a rest.

'There's quite a current in the middle of the river,' Robert said. 'That's making the job hard work for the men.'

'Yes,' the teacher agreed. 'They have to drag the raft with everything on it upriver and then let it be swept back down to where they're unloading on the other side.'

'You can see how strong it is even when they're bringing the logs back empty.'

When the last raft was being packed a porter told Robert it was time for him to climb on and go across the Orange River. The young missionary decided that wasn't for him. Taking off his clothes, and putting them on the raft to be taken over, he walked into the river until he felt the current catching him and then swam towards the other side.

'He'll drown!' one of the porters yelled. 'He won't know that it runs so fast in the middle.'

Several of the men thought the same and they made to swim out to help him. But Robert powered on, taking good account of the current, and was soon on his feet on the other side.

'You're a strong swimmer!' said the teacher, when he arrived on the last raft.

Robert smiled, remembering that when he was an apprentice gardener in Scotland he'd been a strong enough swimmer to safe his friend's life.

It was 26th January, 1818 when Robert arrived in Namaqualand, four months after leaving Cape Town and a year and four months since saying goodbye to Mary. As it was important that things were done in the correct way, he was taken to meet the Chief right away.

'Have you been appointed by the Directors in London?' asked Africaner, in Dutch.

Many times Robert had wondered what their first meeting would be like but it never occurred to him that he'd be asked if he was a real, official missionary!

'Yes,' he answered. 'The Directors of the London Missionary Society appointed me.'

Nearly everyone in the kraal was standing watching the two men. The Chief signalled to some women to come.

'There you must build a house for the missionary,' he said, pointing to a clear piece of ground.

As Africaner had said all he intended saying to the young man, he turned and walked away.

Robert stood and watched, amazed at what was happening right in front of his eyes.

The women gathered long thin branches.

'They might be willow,' he thought, remembering that it was willow logs that were bound together to make the raft.

Using a metal spike they made a circle of deep holes in the ground and then pushed the end of a branch into each one, leaving a small arc of the circle with no branches.

'I imagine that's my door,' Robert decided.

One of the women went inside the circle and the others folded their branches over towards the centre while she reached up to catch them. Holding them firmly, she waited until two of the others joined her inside the circle and bound the tops of all the branches together till it looked just like a beehive from the outside. Then more women arrived with armfuls of grass matting that was woven in and out between the uprights. The young missionary watched his new home being built and it took about thirty minutes from beginning to end! Their job done, some of the builders went back to their own homes, others stirred their fires awake and one or two went off with their children.

There were some disadvantages in living in a home that was more like a beehive than a house and that had been built in half an hour. Robert wrote to Mary and explained what they were.

'I really like my new home,' he told her, 'especially because it means that I can have a little privacy. Not that anyone here seems to want privacy, and people are very happy to appear in my hut beside me at any time of day. But let me tell you what it is like in pouring rain. It's like a riddle. And if you don't know what a riddle is, you should ask your father because he uses one in the garden. It's a coarse sieve like the one I used to use to get rid of gravel from soil at Dukinfield. That's what my home is like – a coarse sieve that only stops sticks from getting through; it certainly doesn't stop the rain! The wind whistles through too. You should hear it!'

Sometime later Robert wrote to her again.

'I occasionally have unwelcome visitors in my little hut. Yesterday I made food to eat and kept some for today. One of the local dogs (they seem to belong to nobody and everybody) came through the wall of my hut while I was asleep and only the sound of it enjoying today's dinner woke me up. Please note it barged through the wall. Most dogs just come in the door space. I'm used to the dogs but I'm not yet used to the snakes. And I'm told that as cattle seem to walk in straight lines, I'm likely to have my home knocked down from time to time by beasts on the move.'

He did, and the same women who built it in the first place, did the job all over again.

Another missionary, his name was Mr Ebner, had worked in Africaner's kraal before Robert moved there. He spent a little while with the new missionary but he wasn't very encouraging.

'Many of the people are very wicked,' he told the young man. 'I've had to put up with terrible things, especially from Titus.'

'Who's Titus?' Robert asked.

'He's Africaner's brother and he hates me with a terrible hatred.'

The young man soon found out that was true. He was in Mr Ebner's little hut one day when Titus stormed in and said the most awful things before cursing him and raging off to swear at someone else. Robert had never heard some of the Dutch words Titus used and he wasn't going to learn them!

Mr Ebner, who was looking forward to retiring and leaving the place, didn't need to tell his colleague how dirty the people were.

'I've never seen any of them wash!' he said.

Now, Robert might not have believed that had he not already been there for some days. He had to agree that unwashed people did not smell very pleasant. Then it occurred to him that he would sometimes be unwashed himself unless it rained. Water was often too precious to waste on hygiene!

'Some of the people have become Christians while you've been here,' the young missionary said. 'Surely they set a good example to the others.'

However, Mr Ebner didn't even have good things to say about some of the Christians.

Until Robert could plant seeds and grow a few things in the dry sandy, stony ground, he lived mostly on milk and meat, though he had to shoot any meat that he ate.

Robert wrote down some things that happened to remind him of what life was like. What follows was written not long after settling under Chief Africaner.

'On more than one occasion after the morning service, I have been so hungry that I have shouldered my gun and gone to the plain or the mountain brow in search of something to eat. And, when unsuccessful, have returned, taken up my Bible and preached at another service. I never liked begging ... but many a time an unknown friend placed some food in my hut and you can imagine how grateful I was better than I can put it into words. I shall never forget the kindness of Titus Africaner, who would often ask what he could do for me. More than once I gave him a few bullets and he nearly always shot something and brought it back to me for food. He was an extraordinary marksman.'

At least Titus was on Robert's side and that made things more pleasant for him than it had been for Mr Ebner. When he did feel lonely, as all missionaries do from time to time, the Scot took his violin out among the rocks and played the tunes he had learned as a boy back home in Scotland. One wonders what his African friends made of that!

Robert Moffat knew his duties; they had already been worked out between the Mission and the Chief. Perhaps that was why Africaner was so anxious to know if the new missionary was there officially. Robert was to hold a service in the morning, a service in the evening and a school for the kraal's children for three or four hours each day. The children had already been taught by Mr Ebner and were ready for their new teacher. But it might have come of something of a surprise to them that hygiene was now part of their timetable. When there was water available, he showed the boys and girls how to wash their sheepskin karosses (blankets).

A little to Robert's surprise, Africaner went to nearly every service! Not only did he go, he listened very carefully.

'He's not what I expected of an outlaw and a murderer,' Robert found himself thinking.

As he listened to what people said about their Chief, he realised that he had been a terrible and terrifying man but that he seemed to be changing. When people change as much as that they are the talk of the town, and Africaner's behaviour was well discussed in his kraal.

'I'm not feeling very well,' Robert thought one day and, as the day went on, he felt worse.

It was very hot and having only meat and milk for food didn't really agree with him and he sometimes suffered for it. This time the attack was really bad. Villagers came and went, each doing what they could to look after their missionary. For two full days he lay in a fever and was quite delirious much of the time.

'Did you see who's in there?' people exclaimed as they looked inside Robert's hut. Chief Africaner was sitting in the gloom beside the young man willing him to get better.

'Did you see his eyes?' one man asked his friend. 'They are full of sympathy and kindness.'

That was not like the Africaner they had known and feared for years. Only when Robert recovered did the Chief leave him alone again.

'Africaner's reading the New Testament,' someone noticed, on a sunny afternoon, and the news buzzed all around the kraal.

The Chief wasn't a brilliant reader, especially in Dutch, but from then on he always carried his New Testament with him and could often be seen reading it.

Robert realised that Africaner had changed and other people commented on it too.

'The one who was like a lion is now more like a lamb,' said a boy in the school.

His friend agreed. 'The Chief who looked for war with other people now wants to talk to them rather than fight. It's not nearly so exciting!'

The young missionary thanked God that there wasn't that kind of excitement and he thanked him from the bottom of his heart when the murdering outlaw Chief Africaner became a Christian. Although his brother Titus didn't say that he trusted in Jesus, he too was a very different man and a really good friend to Robert Moffat.

On the Trail

Some months later Robert harvested the very first wheat from his garden in the kraal. He had sown two hatful's of seed.

'What are these things?' one of his pupils asked, looking at the other plants that were growing.

Pointing to row after row, Robert said, 'This is Indian corn and these are cabbages. The next row is melons and the rest are potatoes.'

When he wrote home to his parents, he told them that after he harvested the wheat he had planted some more right away.

'It's just a trial,' he wrote. 'But I think I might get a second crop in a year. You wouldn't get that in Scotland!'

Robert was a gardener through and through, always willing to experiment with growing things, even if it meant carrying water over very long distances.

Not only did the young missionary have to grow his own food, he had to do nearly everything himself. He must have been very glad that his mother had taught him so well. Perhaps old Mrs Moffat wondered if she had taught him well enough when she read this letter.

'No one can do anything for me in my household affairs. I must do everything which takes so much time that it's hard to do my missionary work. Every day I do a little in the garden and I always seem to be helping to fix broken guns.' There would have been no meat eaten in the kraal without guns! 'I have to be a carpenter, blacksmith, cooper, tailor, shoemaker, miller, baker and housekeeper. ... An old woman milks my cows, makes the fire and does my washing. I do everything else myself.'

Life was, in fact, really hard for Robert. It was really hard for everyone in the kraal because it was not in a good place. Water was scarce and it was difficult to grow food. Robert only managed because he had trained for years as a gardener. Even Africaner was happy to move his family and all his people if a better place could be found.

'But who would want us to live near them?' the Chief asked. 'I was such a troublemaker that other people won't want us within miles.'

Robert understood the problem but he had plenty of time to think about it and pray about it for nothing happened in a hurry.

'I think we should explore the border of Damaraland,' said Robert.

(Damaraland became part of the country that is now known as Namibia).

'Would we be better north-west of here?' Africaner asked.

'It can't be much worse,' the missionary commented, looking at the sand being blown away from his garden and knowing that the second sowing of wheat seed was being blown with it.

There was work to be done before the exploring could start. Robert's wagon was broken again. The young man looked at it and shook his head.

'Its wooden wheels have shrunk in the dry heat and their metal rims have slipped off.'

'Can you fix them?' he was asked.

'I'll try,' said Robert, knowing that there was nobody else to do it.

And how he tried. First bellows had to be made from goat skins (someone else shot the goats!) and then a forge had to be built in order to heat and beat the metal trims for the wheels. There were no pneumatic tyres in Robert's day! However, his inventive mind and clever hands worked well together and eventually, after much hard work, the wagon was ready to roll.

Africaner and Robert didn't go exploring on their own. There were about thirty men, altogether, including Titus. That number was needed to make sure they were safe from attack. And attack was quite likely, for if people saw that Africaner was in the company they might well decide that they were in danger of being attacked and so would go on the defensive.

'Do you have antelopes and giraffes in your country?' someone asked the missionary, as they bumped their way through the desolate countryside.

'No,' Robert replied. 'Nor rhinos nor buffaloes either.'

'But we do have water,' he thought, as he and the other men knelt down beside a stagnant pool that was covered by green froth. All were so thirsty that neither the smell nor the foul taste put them off drinking it. However, for all their searching no place was any better than where they were. The thirty men trundled the wagon all the way back to the kraal.

Africaner considered the problem and decided that they had to move, they had to find another place to live or they would die of malnutrition and drought. A few months after the first trek, Robert plus three members of the Chief's family set off once again, this time on horseback to Griqualand to inspect a piece of land that someone had offered to the people. To spare the horses by carrying anything unnecessary, the men each took only a Bible, a kaross and a water bottle, intending to shoot their food as they went. Riding along the bank of the Orange River they trekked through deep gorges and between overhanging precipices that seemed sky-high as they looked up from underneath them.

'What's that noise?' Robert asked, one day as they rode.

'It's a mighty waterfall,' he was told.

But so utterly exhausted was he that Robert didn't go out of his way to see it, thus missing one of the wonders of Africa! Moffat was not an explorer at heart. He explored to find somewhere to live, not to see colossal waterfalls. Once again their trek came to nothing and Africaner and his people stayed right where they were, fighting against drought and famine as a way of life.

'I have to go to Cape Town,' Robert told Africaner, one day in 1819. 'And I would like you to come with me.'

The Chief looked stunned. 'I thought you loved me and yet you advise me to go to Cape Town! You know I'm an outlaw with a thousand rix-dollars reward on my head. If I went with you, I'd be recognised, caught, handed over to the Governor and executed and someone would be a thousand rix-dollars better off!'

'The Governor will see that you're a different man since you became a Christian,' Moffat explained. 'You even look different!'

There was much discussion on the matter before the Chief trusted his friend and agreed to go with him.

'I'd rather put my head in a lion's mouth!' said Africaner, even after the decision was made.

Such a dangerous exploit had to be planned with great care.

'I think you should travel as my servant,' suggested Robert.

That might not seem such a strange idea to us today, but for a Chief to agree to pretend to be a white man's servant was only possible because Africaner was a Christian and had learned to be humble rather than proud.

When the two men rode away from the kraal as master and servant they were both dressed raggedly for Robert's clothes were now worn through. His mother had taught him how to mend his clothes, but it's not possible to keep things looking decent for ever. Of course, on the way back to Cape Town Robert passed the same homesteads as he had visited on his outward journey.

'Goodness me!' a farmer's wife said, when she recognised Robert. 'Africaner hasn't killed you!'

The missionary smiled, introduced his servant but didn't say who he really was.

'You've escaped his clutches then,' a homesteader announced. 'You're a lucky man!'

Again the missionary smiled, introduced his servant but didn't say who he really was.

'I don't believe it!' another one puzzled. 'Is it really you?'

Yet again the missionary smiled, introduced his servant but didn't say who he really was.

And in one remote homestead the farmer nearly fainted for he thought Robert was a ghost.

'Don't come near me!' he yelled. 'I know you've been murdered by Africaner!'

'I'm not a ghost,' Robert told him.

The farmer wouldn't listen.

'Everybody says you were murdered and a man told me he'd seen your bones!'

Robert spoke to him until he calmed down a bit. Then the farmer asked when the missionary had risen from the dead! Moffat explained that he was alive and that he'd not been killed.

'In fact,' he went on, 'Africaner's now a Christian and no threat to anyone.'

'Well, he was in the past,' said the farmer, and he went on to tell how the Chief had murdered his uncle.

After hesitating for a little while, Robert told the farmer that his servant was none other than Chief Africaner himself.

The man's mouth fell open as he took in what had been said.

'O God, what a miracle of your power!' he prayed aloud. 'What amazing things your grace can do!'

Weeks after starting on their long trek the two men reached Cape Town.

'The first thing I have to do is to take you to the Governor,' Robert told the Chief.

Africaner looked worried. 'So it is,' he said. 'Because if you don't take me to him, someone else will recognise me and have me arrested for the outlaw I am.'

Moffat went to see the Governor, whose name was Lord Charles Somerset. When he explained that Africaner was now a Christian and that he was right here in Cape Town, the Governor looked more than a little surprised, and perhaps more than a little disbelieving.

'I will see him tomorrow,' Lord Charles told Robert. 'And we'll see what happens then.'

The following day Robert and Africaner arrived for their interview. They were shown into the Governor's room and Lord Charles shook their hands and invited them to sit down.

After quite a long conversation Somerset could clearly see there was something different about Africaner.

'It is a great pleasure to see the change in you,' he told the Chief. 'You are certainly not the man you were!'

The outcome of that meeting was not that the outlaw was arrested, imprisoned and executed. Instead, the Governor told Chief Africaner that he wanted to give him a gift of an excellent wagon in which he could travel home … a free man and at peace.

Robert and Africaner were not the only visitors to the London Missionary Society offices in Cape Town. Two others were there from England and they had plans for Moffat.

'We have discussed this in London and with the people here,' they told him, 'and we agree that you should move from Africaner's kraal and spend some months with us visiting the different mission stations in the Colony. After that you are to go to the Tswana people and work with them.' (At that time the Tswana were called the Bechwana.)

This took Robert totally by surprise and, if he thought the Chief would be upset, he was wrong.

'I'll move my family and all my people to the Tswana mission,' Africaner announced. 'That's where we'll settle down and live. The land will be better there and you will still teach us about Jesus.'

Good News!

Missionary matters were not all that was on Robert's mind in Cape Town. Waiting for him when he arrived was a letter from England, a letter from Mary. Her letter, which he received in April 1819, was in reply to one he had written to her in April 1818. It had taken a whole year for one letter to go from South Africa to England and for the reply to come!

Things had changed back home in Dukinfield. Mr and Mrs Smith, recognising that Mary really did love Robert and was sure that God wanted her to be a missionary, decided that their daughter should sail for South Africa. The letter that awaited Robert told him the good news that her parents had agreed to their being married and that she would arrive in Cape Town before the end of the year. Imagine how he felt!

But, and this was a big but, the men from the London Missionary Society told Robert that he was to accompany them on a fact-finding mission and that their travels would take about a year. Robert worked out the dates and discovered that he wasn't going to be in Cape Town to meet Mary when she arrived. Despite that, he and the other two men set off on their travels. No doubt Robert wrote to Mary and explained that someone else would be there to meet her and to look after her until he came back. And we can be absolutely sure that he prayed that his absence would not upset her too much.

God, however, had other plans. The men headed east, visiting mission stations as they went. They stayed at each one, sometimes for a short time and sometimes for longer. It all depended on the state of the work in each station at the time.

'Where do you go from here?' a missionary asked Robert, as they prepared to leave his station.

'Further east still,' he replied. 'We're heading for the borderlands of the Colony and Kafirland. I think our next mission station is to be Bethelsdrop.'

(Kafirland is part of Natal Province and is now known as Zululand.)

As the wagons rolled on towards Bethelsdrop, each time the men stopped they heard rumblings about fighting ahead of them.

'There's war in Kafirland,' they were told, but their wagons trundled on.

'There are always skirmishes,' the men decided. 'It will stop as soon as it started and be over before we arrive.'

That was not to be. The news when they reached Bethelsdrop was serious.

'You'll not get any further east than here,' they were told. 'You'd put your own lives and other people's lives in danger.'

Long discussions were held and it was eventually decided that the fact-finding mission should turn round and head back to Cape Town. There was no point in the men staying on there for it didn't look as if the war was going to come to an end any time soon. The wagons were prepared, the oxen harnessed yet again and the lumbering journey back to Cape Town began. Although the two men from the London Missionary Society were disappointed that they were unable to finish what they went to do Robert must have been eager to get back to Cape Town to meet Mary off the boat!

It was at the beginning of December 1819 that Robert set off to watch for the sails of Mary's boat coming into view. They were married by the end of the year and less than a month later, on 20th January 1820, the oxen were gathered once again and three wagons prepared and packed for the first journey of their married life. Their destination was Lattakoo and the rumbling, trundling, bumping and bruising wagon train would take all of sixty-six days to get there.

Mr Campbell, another missionary who travelled with them, kept a diary of events.

'After passing through Stellenbosch, Paarl and Tulbagh, we wound our way through the Hex River Kloof. The scenery was extremely grand and interesting, being marked by stupendous cliffs, rugged rocks and spiral-topped mountains of great height.'

By day thirteen they had reached the Karroo, a vast area of desert wilderness.

'We are seriously short of water,' Robert explained to his wife. 'So we may have a long trek today for we need to find somewhere the oxen can drink as well as water for ourselves.'

They did reach water that day, but only after fifteen hours of trekking in appalling sun that heated the sand so much that it burned their feet through the soles of their shoes. In those fifteen hours they covered nearly fifty miles. The oxen must have been utterly desperate by the time they drank the little water that was found.

You would think that oxen would be slow ponderous creatures, and so they are most of the time. But two of those that were with them decided that they'd had more than enough of dragging wagons through deep sand. They waited until everyone was asleep and then headed off on their own! Despite the burning wind shifting the top sand their hoof prints could be seen the next morning and one of the porters set off to find and return the runaways. It's hard to imagine it, and the missionaries would have been telling the truth I'm sure, but the man took three days to catch them and get them back and he (and they!) covered about a hundred miles!

On day twenty-nine of the journey they stayed at a remote farmhouse. Mary took the opportunity to write a letter back home to her parents.

'We are all well,' she wrote, 'and my health is extraordinary. It is true I feel a little feeble in the hottest part of the day, but I'm not as bad as I was at home in warm weather.' As Mary wrote, she wondered what her mother would think when she read that, 'It is frequently one or two in the early morning when we stop our travelling ...'

'What do you think of our country?' asked a farmer's wife, as they stopped and stayed at her home.

Mary smiled. 'The people are wonderful,' she said. 'I've never met with such kindness before. We are welcomed into every home we visit.'

The farmer's wife smiled. 'Of course, we welcome visitors!' she laughed. 'We have so few of them! But what do you think of the country itself?'

'I've only seen from Cape Town to here,' explained the English woman, 'and I'm amazed at the Karroo. It's a perfect desert.'

Mr Campbell, who was listening to the conversation, added 'You would need a good pair of spectacles to see a blade of grass in the Karroo.'

After stopping at Beaufort West, the wagon train had to climb over an amazingly steep part of the country.

'How on earth will we get up there?' Mary asked her husband.

Robert looked at the track and asked himself the same question. But the porters who were travelling with them knew what to do.

'We'll take the wagons up one at a time,' their leader said. 'And we'll use as many oxen as it takes to drag each one up.'

It took twenty-two of their strongest oxen to drag the first wagon up to the top of the ridge. Then they brought the beasts down, harnessed them to the second wagon and dragged it up to the top. The oxen needed a long rest before they were taken, unwillingly, down again to the bottom to trundle the last wagon the long steep climb to the top.

'They may not be as handsome as English cows,' Mary said. 'But these oxen are strong creatures.'

Robert burst out laughing. 'I think we need strength rather than beauty here.'

The ox right beside them snorted, making Mary jump, and she laughed too.

Without saying a word aloud, the missionary thanked God that his wife was the kind of woman who could laugh despite all the difficulties she was meeting day by day. However, Mary looked serious when they reached the last farm in the Colony for they heard that the farmer had killed twenty-eight lions in the first month after he and his family settled there.

Eventually the wagon train reached the Orange River.

'How will the porters get us across there?' Mary asked, looking at the depth of the water and the speed at which it was flowing.

Robert was amazed at his wife. She had developed such as respect for the porters that she thought they could do anything. But even they couldn't get the wagons through the torrent. They had to trundle for three days upstream before they reached a ford they could cross safely.

From the Orange River they went to Griqua Town and eventually to Lattakoo, arriving there on 25th March 1820, having spent sixty-six days on the trail. Missionaries had worked at Lattakoo before and Mary was pleased at what she found. There was a church building that could hold about 400 people and a row of simple houses for the missionaries, each with its own garden. Of course, they needed gardens to grow their own food. It was just as well that Robert was a trained gardener.

A week or two later the Moffats discussed life in Lattakoo so far.

'I wish more people would come to church,' Mary said. 'Some weeks it's nearly full and other weeks it's nearly empty.'

'But there's one person who is always there,' reminded Robert. 'Our old blind woman loves Jesus so much that she never misses church.'

Mary's heart warmed as she thought of the woman. Being blind didn't stop her smiling when she spoke about the Lord Jesus.

'Do you think we should start a school for girls?' her husband asked. 'It seems a pity only to teach the boys.'

'I'm not sure if it's worth it,' the young woman thought aloud. 'Women seem to do all the work here and the girls start working when they are very young.

I don't think they would have any time to make use of reading and writing.'

'It would help if we could speak the language,' Robert told his wife. 'I know the Africans understand Dutch, but they don't think in Dutch.'

'And neither do I,' announced Mary. 'Are you suggesting that I start learning Tswana?' she asked. 'And try to master Dutch at the same time? I don't think I could do that.'

(Tswana was then called Sechwana.)

Robert shook his head. 'No,' he said. 'You concentrate on Dutch just now. But from now on I'm going to try to learn Tswana.'

The missionary was true to his word. From that day he worked as best he could at learning the local language but he had so little time that it was very, very slow going.

Mary had heard a great deal about Africaner and met him only once when he arrived at the mission station with articles and cattle belonging to Robert that had been left at the Chief's kraal. The former thief returned every single item that his friend had left and it had all been well looked after. When the time came for the two men to say goodbye they hoped it would not be for long as Chief Africaner still intended bringing his people to live nearby. But that was not to be for the Chief died shortly afterwards and his people stayed where they were.

While the Scot wasn't there when his friend died, Robert heard what happened and that comforted him.

When Africaner knew he had not much more time to live, he gathered his family and his people all around him.

'We are not what we were – savages,' he told them. 'We are people who say that we believe the gospel. Let us then live in peace with all men, if possible. And, if it is not possible to live in peace with some men, you should go to your elders and discuss the problem before taking any action.'

What advice from a former murdering outlaw!

Then he went on to tell them that they should stay together. 'And treat any missionary as one sent from God,' he told the people, who must have been sad when they realised they were hearing his last words. 'I have great hope that God will bless you when I have gone to heaven. I feel that I love God,' Africaner told them. 'He has done so much for me and I didn't deserve any of it.'

Chief Africaner reminded his family and all his people what he had once been like and how he knew that through Jesus Christ he was forgiven and would go home to heaven. Not long afterwards Robert Moffat's friend died and saw Jesus face to face.

The Eight-day Loaf

After some comings and goings, Robert and Mary Moffat eventually settled in Lattakoo in May 1821, by which time they had a baby girl, also called Mary. They were not the only Europeans there as others came and went over the years. The missionary who was with them at the beginning learned a lesson the hard way.

'I just can't believe what's just happened,' he told Mary. 'My bread's been stolen.'

'I'm so sorry,' his friend said. 'But the people steal anything that's not nailed down.'

'But my bread ...,' moaned the young man. 'How could they steal my bread?'

Now, if you are wondering what all the fuss was about, perhaps you'll understand when you realise that it really was HIS bread. The missionary had dug the soil and raked it. He'd planted the seeds and watered the shoots. After watching the grain grow and ripen, he'd gathered the heads of corn and threshed away the chaff. Then he'd put the seeds, a little at a time, between two grinding stones and turned the stones round and round and round until he had rough flour to make bread. After that he'd made bread dough and kneaded it before leaving it to rise. Then he'd shaped the dough into a loaf that was big enough to feed him for eight whole days. Finally, he baked the loaf, smelled the delicious goodness of it and put it on a shelf in his house to cool when he went out to work. But when he came home there was only the smell of his bread left, for someone had forced open the window, climbed in and stolen his loaf, the only food he had for the next week. No wonder he was upset.

Of course, water is needed if anything is to grow and nobody knew that better than Robert, the professional gardener. So that their food would grow a ditch was dug from the river to the missionaries' gardens. It was a huge dig, for the ditch was about three miles long!

'Look at that!' laughed Robert, one dry day.

The water from the river had trickled along the ditch to the gardens and, although everywhere else was dry as could be, the new seedlings that were growing were doing well for the soil around their roots was kept damp.

'It was worth all the effort,' Mary agreed, giving her baby a hug. 'By the time little Mary's old enough to be eating them, there will be plenty of vegetables for her to enjoy.'

But a day or two later, when Robert went to inspect his seedlings, they were looking very poorly. Putting the palm of his hand on the soil he discovered that it was bone dry.

'What's happened?' he wondered, walking along the ditch. 'Has the wall caved in and caused the water to dam up between here and the river?'

With spade in hand, the missionary began walking along the ditch, checking for a sandy avalanche. But there was none. Some village women had seen the irrigation scheme and had decided to join in. So they dug ditches from his one and led the water into their gardens so there was none left for the missionaries!

'What do we do about that?' Robert and his colleague asked each other. 'The people need to water their gardens just as much as we do.'

The two men decided on a plan. They would let the water flow into the villagers' gardens until they were watered. Then, in the hottest part of the day when everyone else would be resting in the shade, they would go out and divert the water back into their ditch and allow their seedlings to be watered. And that's what they did ... nearly every single day, for the villagers just undid their work as soon as they discovered what had been done.

One day Robert was out in the bush when he saw some men from a nearby village digging a grave. He watched as they worked, noticing that two small children were sitting nearby.

'Poor mites,' he thought, 'having to sit there and watch someone they love being buried.'

Then a shocking thought zipped into his mind. Was it their mother who had died? If it was, the children were in terrible danger. The custom there at that time if a mother died, was to take her children to her grave and bury them — alive, or leave them to be eaten by wild animals!

Robert watched the scene being worked out before him. The grave was completed and the body was lowered into it. Then two men took the terrified children and were about to put them in the grave when the missionary showed himself. He pled for their lives, but two small motherless children were of no value at all.

'Why should we save them?' he was asked.

'Their mother is dead. See, there she is,' one man said, pointing to the still-open grave. 'There's nobody to look after them.'

'Give them to me,' Robert pled, appalled at the thought of them being smothered by sand as the grave was filled in.

'You!' laughed an elder. 'Will you look after the children?'

Robert said that he would, that he and Mary would care for the children as their own. The men held a discussion in Tswana and then handed the two little ones, a girl and a boy, to the strange white man who just didn't understand how things worked in their country.

We don't know what Mary said when her husband arrived back home with two wee ones. But she became a mother to them and they were part of the Moffat family from then on. Shortly afterwards Mary had another baby, a second little girl, and they called her Ann. The family was growing!

* * *

Much of the missionaries' time was spent working with their hands. They gardened and looked after their few animals. And they hunted and made any furniture they needed and mended their tools and their shoes. In fact, if something needed to be done, they had to learn how to do it. There were no bakers or butchers, no carpenters or decorators, no farmers or blacksmiths apart from the missionaries. They had to do everything themselves.

All the time left over from the things that absolutely needed to be done was spent teaching and preaching, reading the Bible to those who couldn't read, helping the people to sort out their differences without going to war and trying to live godly lives that others could copy.

'There's a serious shortage of water,' the Chief told Robert, in the height of the dry season, 'and the village elders have decided to call in a rainmaker.'

The missionary was disappointed to hear that. He knew that only God could send rain. No magic spells could make rain clouds gather and showers begin.

Mary described the rainmaker in a letter to her family in England. They would certainly never have seen one in Dukinfield!

'The man arrived with a leopard skin wrapped around him and monkey tails dangling from his waist. He was wearing a headdress of ostrich feathers and his face was painted.'

As soon as the rainmaker appeared he began to make demands.

'Give me sheep and goats and the rain will fall.'

The people, who were poor and couldn't afford to give their animals, had no choice and did so.

A few drops of rain did fall that day, but only a few drops.

'That's all the rain you get for being so mean and only giving me sheep and goats. If you give me oxen, the rain will fall,' they were told.

Hard as it was, the people gathered together and gave the trickster oxen. But no rain fell. Once again the rainmaker pretended it was all the people's fault.

'It's because you're not giving me enough,' he snorted. 'Give me the heart of a lion and then the rain will come.'

The village men went off into the bush and it seemed such a long time before they eventually came back with a lion's heart. But still no rain fell. And none fell when he demanded, and was given, a baboon. He had told them the baboon had to be perfect and then he pretended to find hairs missing from its tail!

The village people were getting really angry and the rainmaker knew it. He decided to play an even crueller trick on them.

'It's the bell on the white man's church that's scaring the rain away. You'll never have any rain while the bell tolls or while the white men are here. Even if rain clouds come, they'll see their white faces and hear their bell and be scared off by them.'

Then, as a final strange effort, the rainmaker blamed the salt that the missionaries used in their cooking!

That night Robert, Mary and their fellow workers met to pray. Words from the Bible calmed their minds. And the words were, 'The Lord of hosts is with us; the God of Jacob is our refuge.'

They went to bed that night trusting that God would keep them safe from the lies of the rainmaker and the fear and anger of the people.

The next day the atmosphere in the village was ugly. Robert went to the Chief.

'The rainmaker could not bring rain because he's a man and not God,' he told him.

The village elders were so angry with the rainmaker that Robert realised they might even kill him.

'He's stolen our sheep and goats! He's eaten our oxen! He's wasted our time hunting for a lion and a baboon and there's still no rain!' they yelled.

The people were desperate.

'Our children are going to die. Look at them!' he roared, pointing at some boys and girls who were lying listlessly in the shade, their stomachs swollen for want of food or drink.

The elders gathered in a circle and began to talk seriously and quietly. Because they were speaking in Tswana Robert couldn't understand all they were saying, but he could work out from their faces that they were making plans.

One of the elders strode over to Robert some time afterwards. The missionary was in the middle of fixing a wagon.

'I have an important message to give you,' the man said.

All the white people were called to be there at the same time and Robert and his colleague stood together, both praying silently as they waited to see what would come out of this ugly scene. The elders all gathered round and nearly enclosed Robert and Mr Hamilton in their circle. And it seemed that all of the rest of the village had gathered outside of it.

'We, the chiefs of the village,' an elder said, 'have decided that you will leave the country. You have not kept our traditions. You have brought all kinds of trouble to us. If you don't go ...' and what was said was not good.

The two missionaries stood still, watching the Chief, whose spear was quivering in his right hand. Mary, who was standing at the door of her home with baby Ann in her arms, watched and prayed.

Robert stepped forward. 'We do not want to leave. In fact, now more than ever we know we should stay here, right where we are. If you have decided to get rid of us, you will have to take strong measures.'

The village elders listened angrily, the spear still quivering in the Chief's hand.

'You may spear us or burn us out,' said Robert, his voice still strong. 'But we know that you won't touch our wives and children.'

With that, Moffat pulled his clothes open, exposing his chest.

'If you will, you can drive your spears into my heart. And if you do that, my companions will know that the time has come for them to leave.'

The Chief's hand firmed on his spear and he stabbed it into the ground.

'These men must have ten lives,' he said. 'That's what makes them so fearless of dying. Perhaps they are right and there is life after death.'

That night, as Robert tried to relax before sleeping, a thought kept going round in his mind.

'It would make all the difference if I could speak Tswana,' he thought. 'Then the village elders and I would really understand each other. They and we only speak Dutch with our mouths; we don't speak it with our minds and hearts.'

Robert had been working at the language, but he knew he wasn't fluent. He decided that he really needed to take drastic steps to learn Tswana.

Wars and more Wars

While the Tswana people, with whom the missionaries worked, were mostly peace-loving who just wanted to be left alone to grow crops and look after their animals, not everyone in the area was like that. Some of the people groups wanted to drive the Tswana out of their homelands and take them over. One group, the Mfengu (then known as the Mantatees), were about to cause no end of trouble. Rumour often reached Lattakoo that the Mfengu were on the march, and most of the time nothing came of it.

'I would like to visit Chief Makaba and his people,' Robert said to the village elders.

They lived about 200 miles to the north-east.

'No,' he was told. 'There is news that the Mfengu are on the move and heading in this direction. It's not a good time for you to go away on such a long journey.'

Robert, who had heard so many rumours about the Mfengu over his time there, decided that he should go anyway as the rumours never came to anything.

'I forbid any of our men from going with you,' the Chief said.

That's why Robert headed off for such a long journey with just a few men who worked for the missionaries. Travel was slow and difficult.

After some days on the journey, the travellers heard news of the Mfengu. It seemed that they were only twenty miles from Lattakoo. Four days later the news was even more serious.

'We'll have to go back right away,' Robert told his men. 'And we need to move quickly.'

They did, and arrived home with the news that the village was likely to be invaded, and soon!

Did the Chief tell Robert that he had been really stupid to disobey him and head off on such a long journey? No, he did not!

'I am exceedingly thankful that you were so hard-headed,' he told the missionary. 'You have discovered our danger in time to do something about it.'

And what they did about it was send for reinforcements from Griqua Town to come and help them defend their land.

The Griquas arrived just on time and the missionaries prayed with the people, asking that God would defend them against the Mfengu and that they would be left in peace to live in their homelands. About a hundred horsemen, Griquas and villagers, prepared to ride out to meet the Mfengu, hoping to persuade them to talk rather than fight.

'Will you come with us?' the leader of the troop asked Robert. 'At least you know some of the language.'

Had it not been such a tense time the missionary would have been delighted that his language study was beginning to pay off.

'I'll come,' he agreed, pulling himself on to his horse.

That day they rode about halfway to the Mfengu. The following morning a small group, including Moffat, rode on until they came in sight of the invaders, whose axes and spears glinted in the distance. As the men rode on they came to a young Mantatee woman, wretched and starving. The men pulled their mounts to a halt and held a brief discussion.

'We'll give her some food and then send her back to her people with a message saying we want to talk rather than fight,' they decided.

The woman gulped down the food she was given and did as her helpers asked. With more food in her hands to eat as she walked, she headed back to her people with the message. Moffat and the other men watched to see what would happen.

'She's nearly there,' one said.

'Look,' another pointed. 'They're gathering round her. She must be telling them what we said.'

A few minutes later they knew exactly what the Mfengu thought of their suggestion. They could see them brandishing their spears and axes in the air. They were not in any mood for talking!

Later that day, when still in sight of the invaders, Moffat and the men found an old man and a boy, also

Mfengu and also starving of hunger and near to death. In full view of their enemies, and hoping they were being seen, they fed the pair and cared for them. The distant raiders saw what was happening and once again brandished their arms.

'They're not going to talk to us,' one of the Griqua chiefs told Moffat.

'You're right,' the missionary agreed. 'They're warriors and they're out to fight.'

The following day the battle began. The Mfengu, armed with their traditional weapons, raced forward with a spine-chilling howl. When they had no choice but to fight back, the Griqua and Tswana raised their guns and began to fire. For two-and-a-half hours the conflict raged. You would think that javelins, war axes, spears and clubs would be quickly outmatched by guns, but the Mfengu were ferocious warriors and knew what they were doing. They were, however, eventually overcome.

Another village had sent men to fight with the Griqua against the Mfengu and they fought with poisoned arrows. As soon as the archers saw that their enemies had been defeated and were on the run, they chased after them to their camp and started firing poisoned arrows there, mostly hitting women and children who had not run away. Seeing what was happening, Robert, who was not taking part in the battle, rode as fast as he could into the Mantatee camp. The archers saw him coming and lowered their arrows, not wanting to kill the one who was doing his best to save them!

'It was while I was trying to stop them firing at the women and children that I nearly lost my own life,' he told his wife afterwards.

'What happened?' she asked, perhaps unsure that she really wanted to know.

'I got hemmed in between a high rock on one side and some Mfengu on the other. There was just a narrow passage and I had to get through it.'

'And then what happened?' said Mary.

'Out of nowhere, right in the narrowest part of the passage, a Mantatee rose up blocking my way. He'd been shot and had nothing to lose by killing me even if he died in the effort. His blade was raised and I'd no way of escape. By the time I could have turned he'd have hacked me to death.'

Seeing that he was fine, Mary asked what happened next.

'A Griqua behind me saw that I was cornered and fired his gun so accurately that I felt the bullet whizz past my head before it reached its mark and the Mantatee landed at my feet. Poor man.'

Although Robert could have done nothing for the man, it didn't feel good to know that the warrior had been killed to save his life.

The Mfengu women and children who were left when the menfolk ran for their lives were treated kindly. Many were injured, most were starving, and all who would go were gathered up and taken back to the mission station at Lakattoo.

'The Mfengu will attack us because the women and children are here,' some villagers thought.

Others doubted that. 'They won't risk it.'

'They'll think they're all dead,' one of the elders suggested. 'And they would have been if the missionaries hadn't brought them here to be fed and have their injuries treated.'

Rumours of Mfengu coming to attack were so frightening that some of the villagers buried their special things and headed off to the nearest town for safety. But no attack came. The warriors had gone and the villagers came back to live in their homes in safety.

The following year Robert and Mary Moffat had to go to Cape Town and they took the Chief's son along with their own children. His name was Peclu. Another of the village chiefs went with them.

'You should see the country of the white man,' Chief Mothibi told his son.

And what stories he had to tell when he came home. Peclu had never seen the sea before and it was a great surprise to him.

'Ah ga si khatla?' he asked in astonishment,' when he saw a ship's boy climb up the rigging of a sailing ship in the harbour at Cape Town.

Robert laughed. 'Ah ga si khatla?' means 'Is that an ape?'

'No,' said the missionary, 'That's not an ape. That's a boy climbing up there.'

Peclu looked at the ships, totally unable to work out what they were.

'Do these water-houses unyoke like wagon oxen every night?' he asked.

We don't know how Robert answered that question. The boy's next query was easier to answer. 'Do they graze in the sea to keep them alive?' Or maybe it wasn't easy to answer than one either!

When they returned to Lakattoo the Chief's son had things to tell that his father could never understand. How do you explain a ship to someone who doesn't know what the sea is like?

But one thing that Chief Mothibi and the elders did understand was that Lakattoo was not the best place to live. So, after much discussion and exploring of the countryside for miles around, it was decided that they should all move a few miles away to Kuruman, where water always flowed. (Kuruman is in the North Cape Province of South Africa.) And by the time they moved they were glad to get away from many unhappy memories. For 1824 was another year of battles and bloodshed, terrible weather conditions and failing crops. And it was in 1824 that Peclu died, the Chief's son who had had such fun in Cape Town. Robert and Mary understood what it was like to lose a son for their baby boy died that year too when he was just five days old. The Chief's family and the missionaries understood each other's loss.

* * *

It was very hard indeed, but Robert Moffat did study the Tswana language. It's difficult to work out where he found time to do that. But he did. Not only that, but he translated little bits of the Bible into Tswana as well as making up a spelling list and a Bible question and answer booklet.

'That's the booklets ready to go off to be printed,' he told his fellow missionaries, before he sighed with relief.

'It shouldn't take them too long to do that in Cape Town,' one replied. 'There's a printing press there. And they know how much we need them.'

Time passed and the books didn't come. More time passed and the books still didn't come. And yet more time passed and Robert wrote to ask what had happened to them. To their amazement the translation papers had been sent to England to be printed. That meant they would take ages! Sometimes God's people have to be very patient even when they don't understand why things happen the way they do.

'Mary,' said Robert, one day, 'You know how I feel about the Tswana language. I've managed to learn a lot and can speak much better now. But I need to live with Tswana people for a time to really understand. And I need to really understand before I can start translating the Bible into their language.'

It was hard for Mary Moffat. Although she put on a brave face, she really didn't like when her husband went away. Apart from finding it hard to be without him, she knew that travelling was very dangerous, and when he left she might never see him again.

It was agreed that Robert Moffat would go to a lonely place some six days trekking away and that he would stay with a young chief there, living as one of his family for ten weeks. He would hear neither English nor Dutch there and so would have to learn Tswana the hard way.

It worked! When Robert returned home three months later he spoke and understood Tswana almost like a villager. But imagine poor Mary Moffat when he told her what had happened on his travels.

'It was dark and we didn't have enough wood to keep the fire going. Trying to keep out of sight of men or beasts, I crept among the bushes to the side of a pool. I had not gone far when I saw between me and the sky four animals looking right at me, probably because I'd cracked a stick as I crept. On looking closer I found that the large, round, hairy-headed visitors were lions and I retreated on my hands and feet towards the other side of the pool. When I came to my wagon driver I found him looking in the opposite direction where two lions and a cub were eyeing us both up. Thankfully the lions had prey and we huddled together in our wagon listening to them munching their way through the animal they had killed, just very grateful that we were not on their menu.'

Thankfully, Mary didn't hear that story until her husband was safely home!

Tswana in Print

Now that Robert Moffat could speak Tswana, he looked for ways of putting the language to use.

'No more sacks in sermons,' Mary laughed, after her husband had preached to the people in their own language.

Robert shook his head.

'No more sacks,' he agreed, smiling.

A visitor, who didn't know what they were talking about, looked so puzzled that the missionary explained.

'I used to preach and then a translator changed it into the language of the people. I didn't know the language well enough to preach, but sometimes I knew enough to be quite sure that the translator was making mistakes. I suspect that, if he couldn't think of the translation quickly, he just said whatever came into his mind. For example, one day I said that our salvation is very important and I heard him translating "very important" as "a very big sack". No wonder the villagers were confused when they heard that salvation was a very big sack.'

Their visitor smiled. 'I can understand why you had to learn Tswana,' he said. 'What I don't understand is why it took you so long to do it. After all, you've been in South Africa for nearly ten years.'

Mary said that they'd been so busy that there was no time for language study.

Her husband looked thoughtful.

'You're quite right,' he said. 'I let being busy stop me from doing what was really, really important. I just hope and pray that God spares our lives here for a long time so that I can put the language to good use.'

God answered that prayer because the Moffats continued to work there for more than forty years.

The spelling book, which had been sent to Britain for printing, arrived at the mission station.

'Now we'll be able to start a school where the children learn in Tswana rather than Dutch,' the missionaries decided.

Plans were made and the school started.

'It's great for our children to learn in their own language,' an elder said to his friends.

Another agreed. 'Yes. It always worried me that Tswana children who went to school had to learn everything in Dutch. It felt as though their minds were being stolen away from us. I was afraid that one day the old language would be forgotten and that our children's children's children would think they were Dutch and not Tswana at all.'

The Chief, who had been listening very carefully, spoke.

'That was my fear too,' he admitted. 'If a child begins to think in another language, he will be lost to his people.'

'Do you think Mr Moffat will ever think in Tswana?' wondered the first elder.

Smiling, the Chief said that he was sure that their friend was trying to do just that.

'I still don't know why the missionaries love us enough to do all they do for us. Over the years our people have stolen their crops, diverted their water supply, taken things from their homes and even laughed at them. Yet all they've done has been for us. Now Mr Moffat has taken something from us. He's taken our words, our speech, and made them his own.

When they told Robert what they were thinking, he was very quick to explain that he loved them because Jesus first loved him.

'You think it amazing that we came from another country to live with you and to tell you about the Lord Jesus,' he said.

The elders agreed that it was truly amazing.

Robert continued. 'Then think how amazing it is that Jesus came from his home in heaven to earth to show us what God is like and that he loves us.'

Nodding in agreement, the elders listened to every word. Some of them were beginning to understand.

'Not only that,' said the missionary. 'You think it's amazing that we live to help you. The wonderful truth is that Jesus lived and died to save you from your sins.'

Thinking back to when they stole from the missionaries, when they harmed them and when they took their water, the elders began to wonder if perhaps they might be sinners after all.

When Robert was telling his fellow missionaries about his talk with the elders, they all knew for sure that only when speaking in Tswana could a conversation like that be held.

'Talking in their language reaches parts of their minds and hearts that Dutch will never reach,' he told Mary. 'I'm just very sorry that it took me so long.'

'You can't change the past,' his wife told him. 'But you can make a difference to the future.'

One of the other missionaries at Kuruman suggested that, as Africans love singing, Robert should write some hymns in Tswana. He did, and his Tswana friends thought they were great!

For nearly ten years Robert, Mary and the other missionaries who worked with them had seen very little difference in the lives of those they hoped would become Christians. That didn't stop them teaching the children in school, taking services, caring for the sick and trying to keep the peace. Nor did it stop Robert producing food in his garden, making and mending his tools and those of the villagers too and also keeping everyone's guns in good order. Wild animals, shot in the chase, formed a tasty part of the people's diet.

'I wonder if we'll ever see this building full,' Robert said, as he and his fellow workers put the finishing touches to a little church at Kuruman.

It was May 1829, and the new building was to be the school and meeting place as well as the church for some time afterwards.

'That's what we're praying for,' his friend replied. Just a few weeks later, on the first Sunday of July, they saw their prayers answered. While the church wasn't full of new Christians, it was full of local people who had come to see six of their friends stand up in public and say that they believed in the Lord Jesus Christ. The new Christians and their missionaries then took the bread and wine of Communion together to remind them that Jesus died to save them from their sins.

God sometimes does very special things for his people, and he did a very special thing for Mary Moffat that weekend. Two years before, sometime in 1827, she had a letter from a friend in England asking if there was anything useful she could send to Kuruman. Of course, her letter took a long time to come by sailing ship, wagon and runner. Mary thought about it and then wrote saying 'Send us Communion dishes (goblets for the wine and a tray for the bread) for we shall want it someday.' Mary's letter took months to travel back to England. When it arrived her friend bought Communion goblets and a tray, packed them very carefully and then sent the parcel on its long, long journey to Africa. Guess what! The parcel arrived on the first Saturday of July 1829 two years after Mary wrote asking for the Communion dishes, and the very day before the first Tswana Christians at Kuruman were to take their first Communion!

July 1829 marked a real change at the mission station, and it showed in all sorts of ways.

'I can't believe that the women want a sewing school,' Mary laughed delightedly. 'They've never shown any interest in clothes before.'

The sewing school started, but the women who came were so impatient to see their new clothes that they wore them before they were finished!

'It's hard not to laugh,' eight-year-old Mary told her mother, 'but I've just seen a man walking around in a jacket that only has one sleeve.'

Robert grinned. 'That's nothing. When I saw him yesterday, it had no sleeves and he was wearing it upside down.'

'I wonder what the folk back home at Dukinfield would say about my class,' his wife said. 'But clothes made of different bits of cloth that don't match each other are quite the fashion with the women and girls here. They make ordinary English clothes look dull by comparison.'

Mary and Ann were not the Moffats' only children. There was also Robert, who died as a baby when they lived at Lakattoo. Then a second son was born. He was also called Robert. Other boys and girls soon joined the family: Helen, Elizabeth, James, John, Elizabeth and Jean – ten in all before their family was complete.

Of course, there were no shops selling cloth at Kuruman and the women had to find whatever they could to sew with. Animal skins were the perfect solution, especially for the men who wanted to join the class. Soft leather trousers were very popular, even if the fit was sometimes a little unusual. And now that they were wearing clothes they had made, the people didn't want to get them in a mess. Before that, they had rubbed animal fat all over themselves. Many stopped doing that and used the fat to make candles instead. When others saw the candles and discovered the difference having a light in the dark made to their lives, they started making them too.

Anyone visiting Kuruman could see the difference that wearing clothes and having candles made to people. But the difference that the Moffats were best pleased with was in the lives of those who trusted in Jesus. They had waited and prayed for such a long time for this to happen, and it did.

Around that time one of the new Christians was near to death, and she knew it.

'Why is she so happy?' some people asked.

They didn't understand that the woman knew she would soon be with Jesus in heaven.

'I am going to die,' she told the people, who were weeping and wailing all around her. 'Don't weep for me. I'm not going to die like an animal. I'm going to be with Jesus.'

Her family and friends listened to what she had to say because, wherever you are in the world, last words are very precious and important.

'Weep for your own sins and souls,' she told them.

They would remember that.

While her funeral was sad, because it is always sad to say goodbye to someone you love, it was also joyful because the Christians there knew that the woman was with Jesus and could see him face to face.

Chief Moselekatse

Some months after that two messengers arrived at Kuruman.

'Who are you?' they were asked by the Chief.

'We are Ndebele,' they said, giving the name of their people group. 'And we come with a message from Moselekatse, the king of our people.'

(The Ndebele were then known as the Matabele.)

'Do you come with a message of peace?' the Chief wanted to know, for the Ndebele were known for their fierceness.

Some said they were even more warlike than the Mfengu!

'Our message is one of peace,' he was told.

The men were welcomed and fed the best of the food in the village. That was important in their culture. If the message was of peace there was time to welcome the men properly before hearing what they had to say. And what they had to say was very, very surprising.

'King Moselekatse has sent us to learn about the teaching of the white men and about the way they live.'

The Chief smiled and declared that 'All messengers should be like this. Mostly they come to declare war! You are welcome as brothers,' he told the travellers.

'And you can spend as long as you want with us here and watch the white men living their lives before you go back home to your king.'

'Thank you,' the men replied. 'That is what King Moselekatse would want us to do.'

That's how two Ndebele men came to be living for a time at Kuruman. They wanted to see absolutely everything in order that they could take a full report back to their king.

'What are these people doing?' Mary was asked by the messengers.

Each of the sewing class showed the Ndebele what they were making. Some proudly pulled on their half-made garments. Even the men showed off their sewing.

Just imagine the Ndebele men seeing trousers for the first time. And can you picture their faces when they saw Robert and the others sitting on chairs around a table and eating from plates with knives and forks? Even the mission station villagers still found that a very funny sight. However, the thing that interested the messengers most was when the villagers met in the church for a service. They only understood a little bit of what was said, but they were fascinated. And the most amazing thing of all to them was that the singing in church was kind and warm and loving. The only time the Ndebele met to sing was when they were going to war and they got themselves wound up to a frenzy by singing war songs!

'You will come back to King Moselekatse with us,' the leader of the two men told Robert.

That was a command rather than a question. When their king told them to do something, they did it immediately. And they expected the missionary to do the same.

As they travelled Robert tried to be like the Ndebele men, he tried to remember what he was seeing as they rode.

'Our wagons went through communities and villages that had been attacked by the Mfengu, or so I thought. Houses had been knocked down and there were human bones everywhere, all scraped clean by wild animals,' Moffat told his fellow missionaries later. 'But it turned out that many of them had been killed by the Ndebele! My two companions were very proud each time we came to where their people had won battles and murdered all their enemies. I must say I wasn't looking forward to reaching their town and meeting their king.'

'What happened when you did?' his colleague asked.

'That's a long story,' replied Robert. 'And I'd like to tell it to you all together.'

Mary and the chiefs sat down, the village elders with them, to hear the missionary's account of his foray into the home town of one of the fiercest of South Africa's peoples. The villagers, not wanting to miss out, also gathered round to listen.

'We rode right into the town,' began Robert. 'And when we reached the centre we came to a huge clearing where animals are kept. Standing round about it, on all sides, and several men deep, were about 800 warriors.'

'Eight hundred!' Mary said shocked at the thought of the danger her husband had been in.

'That's right,' agreed Robert. 'And those were just the ones in the clearing. When I looked round there were more warriors, about two hundred of them behind, on either side of the entry to the town.'

One of the missionaries pictured the situation. 'So you were hemmed in?' he asked.

Robert nodded. 'Totally hemmed in. If I'd put one foot wrong, any one of a thousand spears would have gone through me.'

Mary didn't say anything that people could hear. But God heard her saying thank you that her husband was home safe and well.

Taking a few sips of water, Robert continued his story.

'We were told to dismount. Suddenly the warriors behind us started yelling blood-curdling chants and, as they yelled, they jumped up and down in the most hideous way. They really frightened the horses and I had to hang on to my bridle with all my strength to stop mine bucking. After that the shrieking, jumping warriors circled round in front of us and drew into ranks with the other 800. They are a very highly trained army.'

'What happened after that?' the Chief asked.

'Before I go on I'll tell you what they were wearing. They had on skirts made of ape skins and their legs were covered in the tails of oxen. On their heads they wore feathers, though you could just see the top of their faces for they carried shields that reached up to, and over, their chins.'

The elders were listening intently, some of them open-mouthed.

'They were dressed for war,' one said.

'Or for a welcome ceremony,' suggested another.

Waiting for silence, Robert Moffat continued his story.

'For the next ten minutes there was silence. Nobody moved. The warriors just stood there … waiting. It seemed a long, long time.'

Mary felt sorry that her husband had had to go through such a terrifying experience.

'Suddenly they all started up a war song. Can you imagine the sound of over a thousand men singing and chanting and stamping their feet? It just about made my blood curdle. Then, as suddenly as the singing started, it stopped. I wondered what was going to happen next, when King Moselekatse broke through the ranks of warriors and marched up to us. He had an interpreter with him and we were welcomed by the King. After our welcome, more men came through the rows of warriors and they were carrying all kinds of food and drink.'

'You mean that was an Ndebele welcome ceremony?' the Chief asked.

'So it seemed,' Robert told him, 'for, using the interpreter, the King went on to make a very warm speech of welcome! I have to tell you that I was very, very relieved for I'd no idea what was coming!'

Mary looked at her husband and felt very relieved too.

'What happened after that?' the Chief wanted to know. 'Did the two men who came here tell the King all about us?'

The missionary smiled.

'They were all ready to do that,' he said, 'but when the King saw our wagons he marched off to have a closer look at them. He'd never seen anything like them before.'

The Chief laughed. 'I remember my father telling me about the first time he saw a wagon. He thought it was a new kind of animal!'

'I don't think that King Moselekatse made the same mistake as your father,' smiled Robert. 'He was amazed at the wheels. In fact, he was down on his hands and knees examining them. Then he fired question after question at me through his interpreter. Last of all this question was the one that puzzled him most.

"How did the white man manage to put round the wooden wheel a metal rim that has no beginning and no end?"'

'I don't understand,' Mary said.

Robert laughed. 'He doesn't have a word for circle,' he explained. 'And he couldn't work out how metal could be made into a circle. Anyway, one of the men who came here answered for me.

"I saw how it was done," he told his King, pointing to my hands. "My eyes saw the hands that did it. He cut bars of iron and beat them into long strips. Then he joined the ends to make them as you see."

King Moselekatse was mystified. "Did he give medicine to the iron?" he asked.

"No," his servant said. "He used only fire and his tools."'

Over the next eight days the two men who had brought Robert to their King told the ruler all they had seen at Kuruman, and about the kindness that had been shown to them there. Robert also had several interviews with Moselekatse.

One day the two men were sitting together talking, the missionary and the King who was known as one of the fiercest and cruellest rulers in South Africa. Moselekatse stretched out his hand and laid it on Robert's shoulder.

'My heart is white as milk,' he said. 'I am still wondering at the love of a stranger who never saw me. You have fed me, you have protected me, and you have carried me in your arms. I live today by you, a stranger.'

The missionary was puzzled. 'I don't remember doing these things for you.'

The king looked at his two messengers, who were never far from his side. 'These are great men,' he told Robert. 'One of them is the greatest Ndebele after me. When I sent them from my presence, it was as if I sent my ears and my eyes and my mouth. It was as if what they heard, I heard. What they saw, I saw. And when they spoke, it was as if I was speaking. They have told me that you fed them, you gave them clothes, and when they were in danger you protected them. What you did to them, you did to me.'

Robert felt that King Moselekatse was speaking from his heart and he told him about the Lord Jesus and how he had even died on the cross to save those who put their trust in him.

A day or two later the two men were talking once again. They weren't alone as some warriors came with the King. They stayed a little distance away and began to sing and chant their war songs, all the while leaping and dancing themselves into a frenzy. Once again, Robert spoke to the King about Jesus.

'Why are you so keen that I should stop fighting wars and killing people?' Moselekatse asked.

Robert looked very serious. 'Look at all the human bones that lie over your country. They speak to me in an awful language. And what they say is that it is wrong, that those who murder will be found guilty by God.'

He then told the King that when Jesus comes back again in glory everyone, good and bad, will rise from the dead, the good to go to heaven and the bad to go to hell. That made King Moselekatse very thoughtful.

The two messengers had been well treated in Kuraman and Robert was just as well treated when he visited the Ndebele. In fact, the King was so kind to him that he sent all kinds of gifts back with Robert in his wagon. Not only that but, when he left, Moselekatse insisted on sending several warriors all the way back with the missionary so that no harm could come to him.

It took Robert Moffat two months to travel from Kuruman to visit King Moselekatse and back. Knowing what a warlike people the Ndebele were, the people in the mission station were very happy to see him home again, especially Mary and their children. What a lot of interesting stories he had to tell them!

Singing ABC

Kuruman began to change when villagers became Christians and some of the changes were obvious. There were the clothes that people made for themselves and wore. While they wouldn't have been found in grand shops in New York, London or Sydney, they were certainly the fashion of the day among the Tswana people. Mary's skill at sewing and her patience as a teacher worked wonders in the local fashion world.

Robert's training and experience as a gardener also made a huge difference to the people. The villagers were used to growing things, but they were also used to crops failing regularly. If they were growing just one crop and it failed, then there was nothing to be harvested and eaten. Robert knew that growing a wide variety of things could mean people having food to eat rather than starving. So he chose the seeds that he thought would grow best and planted them in order that the Chief and elders would see how they grew. Among them were grains like wheat and barley, vegetables like potatoes, carrots, pumpkins and onions along with delicious water melons to cool them down in the heat of summer. Fruit trees were also planted.

'Fruit trees cope much better with drought than ground crops,' he explained to the elders. 'And if you plant nut trees, you'll be amazed at how much grows on them, even with very little rain. Nuts are great food and a few really fill you up.'

Thinking back to their empty rumbling bellies in the hungry years, made the elders take Robert seriously and soon the Kuruman plots were full of good food ripening for the pot. They also grew tobacco which wasn't known to be harmful in those days. They were able to trade their tobacco leaves for money to buy the things they needed that they couldn't make themselves.

'Is that you back at your translation work?' Mary asked her husband, late one afternoon.

'I need to spend as much time on it as I can,' he replied. 'I'm working on Luke chapter 15. Only nine more chapters to go.'

'What a difference it will make to the people to be able to read God's Word for themselves,' thought Mary aloud.

'You've forgotten something,' Robert said. 'So far it's only the children who are learning to read.'

'There are one or two adults too,' his wife reminded him. 'In any case, if the children learn and have books, they'll read to their parents, especially now they have candles to light their homes after their day's work is done.'

Robert went back to his papers. It could take ages to translate even one verse as he needed to be absolutely sure that the right words were used.

It took years rather than months, but eventually the work was done and the entire Gospel of Luke was in Tswana, all written out by Robert's hand and ready to be printed. He also had a small collection of Tswana hymns ready for printing. Today, that would mean sending them off by email to a publisher, but Robert completed the work in the 19th, not the 21st century.

Mary and Robert sat together talking. It was early evening and the children were fast asleep. The candle was flickering and making strange light and dark shapes on their faces. But neither saw the play of the candlelight on the other's face, because they were avoiding eye contact.

'We knew this time would come,' Robert said quietly.

Mary nodded. 'Yes, but that doesn't make it any easier. Does it?'

He agreed.

'I know that Mary and Ann need to go away to school. They've learned as much as we can teach them here,' admitted Mary. 'But Graham's Town is so far away. We wouldn't be able to get to them in an emergency.' She shook her head. 'We'd not even know if there was an emergency until weeks after it had happened.'

'Aren't you forgetting something?' her husband asked.

Trying to smile, Mary said, 'No. Of course, I'm not forgetting that God will be with them and that he loves them much more than we do.'

It was decided that Robert would take the precious translation of Luke's Gospel to Cape Town for printing and that Mary and the girls would travel with him as far as Graham's Town. When they reached there, the two Marys and Ann would spend some time together while he visited the mission stations in the area. That would give young Mary and Ann time to settle down in the Wesleyan School while their mother was still in the area. And it would allow his wife to have a break from travelling before heading on to Cape Town.

'It'll be exciting living in a wagon,' young Mary said, as they prepared to go.

Ann agreed, though she was a bit anxious about being left at school.

'Forget about school just now and enjoy the adventure,' her older sister advised. 'That's what I'm going to do.'

The truth is that, although she was a year older than Ann, she was also nervous about being so far away from home.

Plans were made and things went more or less to plan, the journey to Cape Town via Graham's Town taking from June until October 1830. Almost as soon as they arrived Robert set about finding a firm that could print his translations.

'There isn't anyone in Cape Town who can do it,' he was told, over and over again.

'There must be,' insisted Robert. 'God didn't allow us to get this far with the work for it not to be printed.'

'The only suitable printing press is in the Government Printing Office,' someone said. 'But that's only used for government documents.'

The missionary didn't waste any time and he was soon requesting an interview with the Governor. Permission was granted for him to have the use of the printing press, and that would have been that ... if only there had been printers who could do the Tswana printing. There were none. And printing isn't the kind of job someone can do without training as it is very technical and takes some years to learn. That is, unless you are a very determined Scottish missionary named Robert Moffat and you are desperate to get the work done. He, along with another missionary called Mr Edwards, learned the basic art of printing and the Gospel of Luke and the hymn book were produced. At last! How carefully they were packed for their long journey to Kuruman. And how carefully they were unpacked when Robert and Mary arrived back there, complete with a new baby daughter, in June 1831. They had been away from the mission station for a whole year.

Not only did they bring the printed books back home, they also brought a printing press! Mr Edwards had shipped it to South Africa for the work in Kuruman. If it had come years earlier it would have been of no use at all, because the translation work hadn't been done. God doesn't make any mistakes in the timing of things.

Imagine the Tswana people standing around watching the first printing being done in their village. The press rattled and clattered. It rumbled and shook. But it also did what seemed like magic. Sheets of white paper disappeared in one end of the printing press and came out the other end with lines of black marks all over them. Of course, it wasn't magic, it was ink and the lines of black marks were lines of words – IN TSWANA! One of the elders grabbed a sheet of printed paper and ran right round the village with it.

'It was made in a moment with a round black hammer and a shake of the arm!' he yelled.

Men and women, boys and girls all gathered round to see the amazing sight. And that was the beginning of printing in that part of South Africa.

The work that the Moffats had been doing over the years continued. Robert taught and preached. He fixed guns and wagon wheels. He parleyed with the Chief and elders in Kuruman and travelled hundreds of miles in most directions from there. Mary brought up her children and her Tswana foster children and taught them their school lessons too. Both men and women learned sewing from her and gardening from her husband. And that was how the years passed.

Because they lived in such remote places, missionaries had to be their own doctors. Only when they were seriously ill were they taken to the nearest big town; very rarely did a doctor come to them. One did come at the beginning of 1835. Dr Andrew Smith was travelling to do scientific research and arrived at Kuruman just when Robert needed him most. He was very ill and not getting better.

'I'm glad I'm here,' said Dr Smith, when he saw the missionary. 'This is God's timing.'

Mary agreed and prayed that the doctor would know how to help her husband to get better. He did and, after a time of rest, Robert was back to good health once again.

Just two months later there was another urgent need for a doctor at Kuruman. Mary had had a baby and shortly afterwards she became very ill indeed.

'We know roughly where Dr Smith is working,' said Robert. 'I'll write a letter explaining what's wrong and we can send it with a runner.'

A runner at that time in South Africa really was the postal service of the day. When the letter arrived, Dr Smith left his scientific work right away and rushed back as fast as his horse could carry him. Even though he hurried, it was still many days between the runner leaving and coming back with the doctor.

'Am I on time?' he asked the first villager he met as he neared Kuruman.

'Yes, I think you're on time,' he was told. 'But only just ...'

God did take Dr Smith there on time and he was able to save Mary Moffat's life. There was much singing in the village when she began to get better.

When it was clear that Mary had recovered, Dr Smith had a request to make of his missionary friend.

'I would like to do some scientific work in Ndebele country. But because they are such a warlike people I'd probably not get through their territory alive.'

'That's true,' agreed Robert. 'There is no great change in their lifestyle though we keep praying for God to work in their hearts.'

'I know you are a friend of King Moselekatse,' said Dr Smith. 'Would you consider coming with me? Mary is well enough now for you to go away.'

Robert was so grateful to the doctor, and so eager to see his Ndebele friend again, that it was agreed he should go, even though it would mean being away for three months. Dr Smith's science kept him busy and Robert was just as busy, but he was doing mission work. God really used that time and, because of it, a way opened for American missionaries to work among the Ndebele people. The prayers for the war-lords were beginning to be answered.

* * *

Back home in Kuruman the people were still impressed by the printed page. And they were even more impressed that the children who were at school knew how to read.

'We would like to learn to read too,' the elders told Robert. 'If our children can learn, then their elders can learn. It is not our tradition that our children have knowledge that their elders don't have.'

Those who wanted to learn reading were given spelling books which had long lists of Tswana words in them. But they had to learn the alphabet first before they could sound out the words and discover what they said. Someone found a large alphabet poster and Robert laid it on the ground.

'Sit down and I'll tell you the first letters,' he said.

Of course, the men sat in a circle, which meant that some of them were about to learn the letters upside down!

'This is an 'A',' said the missionary.

The men all shouted 'A' in their loudest voices, which rather startled their teacher.

'And this is a 'B',' he went on, after they repeated A for a while.

Once again they shouted out loudly. 'B! B! B! B! B!'

'Why are you shouting?' enquired Robert, when at last there was silence.

One of the men explained. 'The louder we roar, the sooner our tongues will get used to the sounds.'

Some of the young people in the village had a great idea.

'Teach us the A B C to music,' they asked him. 'We all love singing and we'll learn it more quickly that way.'

Poor Robert. That was seen to be such a good idea that he was half dragged, half pushed into one of the biggest houses in Kuruman, which was immediately crowded with people waiting for him to burst into song! It took him a little while to work out a tune and the one he chose was a Scots song that he'd known since he was a boy.

'Listen to me singing the tune,' he told the crowd, 'and then we'll fit the letters of the alphabet into it.'

The lesson went on and on and on and on. It went on so long that it was after two o'clock in the morning when he managed to escape and go to bed. It wouldn't be true to say that he had much sleep for the singing in the village went on all night – very, very loudly!

Home from Home

'How long ago is it since you left Britain?' someone asked Robert in 1839.

He thought about it for a minute. 'It's over twenty years,' he said. 'In fact, I've spent almost exactly half of my life here in South Africa.'

'Are you looking forward to going home?' was the next question.

The missionary didn't have to think about the answer to that. 'This is my home,' he told his friend. 'I don't know what it will feel like when we get back to Britain. But standing here my feet feel at home on sandy soil and my heart feels at home with the Tswana people.'

'Are you looking forward to being back in England?' Robert asked his wife, as they did their packing for that very long journey.

'I am, in a way,' she replied. 'But not in another. It will be so good to see my father again, but I can't imagine Mother not being there. And, as my two brothers are abroad, we won't see them either.'

Moffat nodded his head. 'I know what you mean. Our families have changed so much in the years since we saw them. Your father and my parents have grown old and your mother and brother have both died.'

'And so have your brother and two sisters,' said Mary quietly. 'And remember, we've changed too.'

The time came for the Moffats to go the long way home to Britain. Apart from anything else, Robert had translated the whole of the New Testament into Tswana and there was nowhere at all in South Africa where it could be printed. So the decision was taken that they should go back to see their families and have the printing done while they were away.

'We'll be able to tell Christians in England and Scotland about the work among the Tswana people,' Mary said. 'And they might be generous and give us money to take back with us. What a lot more we could do if we had money to pay for it. Think of it. We could buy more tree seedlings and plant orchards in the villages.'

The gardener in Robert perked up.

'You're right,' he said. 'Trees are one of the answers to the drought problem. Their roots are deeper and they stay alive for a long time even when there's no rain, which means they crop much more reliably.'

And the craftswoman in Mary was excited.

'If we are given money, I could buy lots of material to take back for the sewing class, and threads and buttons and things.'

Robert laughed. 'What a pair we are! We have weeks to think about it while we are on the boat, and here we are in Kuruman making up a shopping list for England.'

Sadly, when they set sail for England shopping was the last thing on their minds.

'Why can't we go on a steamship?' Ann asked her father, as they set off. 'They only take twenty days to go from South Africa to England. Why do we have to go on a poky troop-ship instead? It takes weeks and weeks and weeks!'

Her father put his arm round Ann. 'I'm really sorry,' he said. 'I would have liked to have done that too. But there isn't a steamship going back just now and we don't know when the next one will be.'

Ann snuggled into her father's side.

'I'm sometimes scared,' she told him. 'There are so many soldiers on the ship and they're so loud.'

'So they are,' agreed Robert. 'But let me tell you about them and then you'll understand. They've been soldiering in China for a time and now they are going home to their families in England. They're just like your mother and me. They're excited about seeing their families again. Maybe that's why they're a bit noisy.'

Ann thought about that and then said, 'You and Mother don't shout.'

Robert tousled her hair and pointed to his other children who were playing a noisy game. 'We don't need to,' he told her. 'You all do it for us!'

The ship hadn't even left port when a very serious thing happened. One of the soldiers came out in spots and then another. Other passengers and crew were sick and the situation was very ugly indeed. It was an especially difficult time for the Moffats because Mary was pregnant and their baby was due to be born. In the midst of the noise and infections of the troop-ship, another little girl came into the world.

'Will she survive this?' her mother wondered, as she cradled the tiny infant in her arms. She did. But just three days later her older brother, Jamie, who was six, died and was taken home to heaven. So there was joy at the birth of one child and deep wounding sadness at the loss of another. Just before he died, Jamie cuddled up beside his mother and talked about heaven where people would always be happy and never again have to say goodbye to those they loved.

Weeks later, as their ship neared the coast of England, the family heard two interesting snippets of news. The first was that their ship was going to dock at Cowes, where Mary had friends. And the second was that the tug that was ordered to tow them up the Thames to London was driven by steam. While they weren't going to be aboard the steamship, that was still very exciting. After nearly three months at sea, they could hardly wait to reach dry land.

'Is that England?' the children shouted.

Almost dancing with excitement they watched as the coast drew closer and ever closer.

'It is,' Mary told them. 'We're nearly there!

'That's Portland Bill,' a soldier said, 'and we'll soon see *The Needles*.'

'What are *The Needles*?' Ann asked.

Her sister Mary looked at her. 'Don't you remember our teacher telling us about *The Needles* before we left?'

Ann grinned. 'I remember! They're a row of huge high chalk rocks off the south coast of England and ships are often wrecked on them.'

Her younger sister looked worried.

'We're not going to be shipwrecked, are we?'

Their father decided this wasn't the time for teasing.

'No, we're not,' he said. 'Let's just stand here and enjoy our first sight of the Isle of Wight.'

'But I thought we were going to England,' said one of the younger children.

'We are,' Robert said. 'We're docking at Cowes, which is on the Isle of Wight, and then we're going on from there to London.'

'Which is the capital city of England,' Ann announced, remembering her school geography.

When they were safely tied up at the quay at Cowes a strange thing happened. Mary and the children left the ship and went to see friends. But Robert, suddenly feeling shy, decided not to disembark and he remained on board. Perhaps he wanted to enjoy the peace and quiet after months of being on a ship with noisy children!

But not long after the excited children had disembarked with their mother a voice was heard calling up to one of the crew.

'Is there a Mr Robert Moffat aboard?'

'Yes, sir,' answered the sailor. 'His wife and children are ashore, but he's on board. Would you like me to get him for you?'

'I'd like that very much indeed,' agreed the minister.

Walking up the gangway behind the sailor, the minister thought about the long journey the boat had come. He was still thinking about it when Robert appeared.

'Good morning, Mr Moffat,' the minister said. 'I heard that there was a missionary aboard ship and thought I should come and welcome you back to your homeland.'

The two men talked together and prayed together before the minister disembarked and went home. In the quiet of his cabin, with his family still in Cowes, Robert thanked God for that good and kind and thoughtful man.

From Cowes the ship sailed along the south coast of England, passing by the white cliffs of Dover on their left and seeing the faraway coast of France on their right at the narrowest point of the English Channel.

'We're turning north now,' Ann said, sometime later. 'See, the sailors are setting the sail in that direction.

One of the crew was passing and heard her comment. Realising that Ann was interested, he pointed out Deal and Broadstairs and said that the name of the next point was North Foreland and after that they'd turn into the great River Thames.'

'Is that where we'll meet the steam tug?' she asked.

'It is indeed,' he replied. 'And none of you will ever have seen one of them before.'

'Oh yes, I have,' said Robert to the children. 'And if you all come round I'll tell you about it.'

The children gathered round their father, for they knew he was a good storyteller. The baby, who was now three months old, was much more interested in her feed.

'When I was eleven years old my family moved from Portsoy, in the north east of Scotland, to Carronshore, which is near the centre of the country. And I remember, just after we moved there, going exploring with a new friend and that's when I saw the most amazing thing.'

'What was that?' young Mary asked.

'It was a steam tug called the *Charlotte Dundas!*'

'I didn't think there was such a thing as a steamship that long ago,' said Ann.

Robert smiled. 'Well,' he said, 'there was. And it was the very first steam tug in the world.'

'Were you on it?' asked the youngest but two Moffat.

'No,' her father admitted. 'In fact, I wouldn't have gone on it if you'd paid me. I remember my friend telling me that it had a furnace aboard that boiled water into steam and that it was the steam that drove the ship's engine. I decided there and then that steam tugs were not for me because I couldn't imagine a boat with a wooden hull would be safe with a furnace on board. My friend said that steamships were the ships of the future. It seems that he was right and I was wrong.'

The Moffat children were fascinated by the steam tug that drew alongside after North Foreland, and they watched as it eased them up the River Thames, which grew narrower and narrower as they reached the great city of London.

'What do you think we'll do while we're in Britain?' Ann asked her older sister, when they were all tucked up in bed on their first night back on dry land.

As neither of them could sleep because they were so excited, they decided to play a game. They would take turns at suggesting things they could do from what they'd heard their parents saying.

'I think we'll meet Mother's father, that's Grandfather Smith,' said Ann.

Mary guessed that they'd meet Grandmother and Grandfather Moffat too.

'But we'll have to go to Scotland to see them,' she added.

'Father says that he's to speak at a great many meetings so I think that we'll move from place to place all the time,' Ann told her sister.

'But shouldn't we be at school?' wondered Mary.

Ann was adamant. 'No, I don't think we should go to school. We'd learn much more by travelling.'

'I'm looking forward to seeing Dukinfield because that's where Father and Mother met,' Mary smiled. 'That would be romantic.'

Ann sat up. 'I'll tell you what I want to see at Dukinfield,' she told her sister. 'I want to see the garden that Grandfather Smith worked in. Father has told me all about it and how different it is gardening in England where there is always plenty of rain.'

'I wonder what it will be like when it rains every day,' said Mary. 'I'm not sure that I'll like that.'

Ann, whose eyes were nearly closing, had the last word. 'We'll need to get umbrellas. I think everyone in Britain carries umbrellas all of the time because it rains all day every single day.'

What a lot the Moffat children had to learn!

'My Name is David Livingstone'

When missionaries are back in their homeland they are often not allowed much of a rest. Instead, they are invited to travel from one place to another to speak at meetings. Of course, in the 19th century, there was no radio or television and missionaries' stories seemed very exotic indeed. People travelled from miles around to attend a missionary meeting. Having been in South Africa for over twenty years, Robert had plenty of stories to tell them.

'Let me tell you about a young woman, who was being held captive by the Ndebele people,' he said, one evening at a meeting.

I was visiting the sick when I met her. And the poor woman was weeping sorely.

"Why are you so sad," I asked her. "Is your baby poorly?" "No," the young woman answered. "My baby is well."

"Is it your mother-in-law?"

"No, no," she told me. "It is not my mother-in-law. My heart is sad for my own dear mother."

"I knew that she was living in her husband's house with her mother-in-law and that she would probably never be free to visit her own mother in her home village ever again. Then I noticed that she had the Gospel of Luke that I had translated into Tswana! The book in her hands was wet with tears."

"My mother will never see this book," she told me through her tears. "She will never hear the good news about Jesus. Neither she nor my friends in our village will ever hear about him. They will die not knowing that he came to save them."

As I watched that poor woman, she turned her eyes to heaven and prayed for her mother. And I joined in her prayer that her mother and her friends in their faraway village would be visited by a missionary and would hear about Jesus and be saved.'

Having told this story to the crowd that had gathered to hear him, Robert explained how important it was that the Bible was translated into all the African languages in order that people could learn to read and then read it for themselves.

'I have translated all of the New Testament into Tswana,' he told the people, 'and one reason we are here in Britain is to have the book printed in time for us to take it back with us when we return.'

People who heard stories like that were very generous and at the end of meetings Robert was often given money for missionary work. Some of that money was used to print the first 500 copies of the Tswana New Testament. When Robert Moffat held the very first one in his hands, his heart was full of joy at the thought of those who would read it back home in Africa, for he had discovered that when he was in Britain he didn't feel at home. His home was at Kuruman.

Mary felt exactly the same. A few months after arriving in England, she wrote to a friend at the mission station.

'I long to get home. I long to see the place where we have worked and suffered for so long. I long to see our beloved companions in the work and to see our African brothers and sisters once again. And I long for my own home. Although we are loaded with the kindness of friends here in Britain, and although we are made welcome everywhere we go, I still long to go home.'

And the home she longed for was in Kuruman, South Africa.

Although there were some railways in Britain by 1840, they weren't usually going to and from the places where Robert was asked to speak. That meant that most of his travels were done by stagecoach, and that was a cold and damp way to travel in the winter. The missionary had forgotten what it was like to be chilled through with damp that didn't lift for days and days at a time.

'You're ill, Mr Moffat,' a doctor told him, before he was about to speak at a meeting one evening. 'If you don't stop and rest for a time, you're going to be so ill that you'll be of no use to anyone.'

Even Robert saw the sense of that and took to his bed till he felt better. But although his body was resting, his mind was rattling on like one of these new-fangled steam trains! Someone had suggested that it would be a good idea to translate the Book of Psalms into Tswana and have it bound together with the New Testament.

'I've already translated about fifty psalms,' Moffat told the person with whom he was staying. 'So I'll use this time off speaking to work on the other hundred.'

His host looked at him. 'I don't think that was exactly what the doctor meant by rest,' he said seriously.

'But I'll be warm and comfortable and not rattling from here to there on a stagecoach!'

Seeing that he had absolutely no possibility of winning the argument, his host did everything he could to provide Robert with a pleasant study in which to work at his translation of the psalms. Despite not really doing what the doctor ordered, he grew strong and healthy once again.

After Robert had recovered and was on his travels once again, he had to call at a house in Aldersgate Street in London. Some young men lived there who were preparing to be missionaries. He was asked to tell them about his work. As he spoke to them, Moffat noticed that one of them in particular seemed interested in every word he said. This young man's eyes never left Robert.

'What's your name?' the missionary asked him, after the meeting was over.

'I'm David Livingstone,' was the reply.

'And I can hear that you're a Scot like myself,' Robert smiled. It was so good to hear a Scots accent in London. 'Where are you from?'

'I was born and brought up in Blantyre,' was the reply. 'And that's just thirty miles or so from your old home in Carronshore.'

The two men talked for a short time before Robert had to leave for another meeting.

Wherever he spoke in London, Moffat noticed that David Livingstone was in the audience. And each time they met, the missionary asked the young man more about himself.

'What are you studying here in London?'

'I'm doing medical studies and I hope that will help me on the mission field.'

On another occasion Robert asked, 'Where do you think God is calling you to go?'

David answered, 'To China. But I can't go there just now because of the war.'

Then one day the two men had longer to talk.

'Do you think I might be suitable for work in Africa?' asked Livingstone.

Robert thought for a while before answering because he knew that what he said was really important and might change the young man's life.

'Yes,' he said. 'I believe you would be suitable for Africa provided you didn't go where the work has been going on for years. You are the kind of person who should be doing pioneering work in places where the good news about Jesus has not yet reached.'

David's heart raced when he heard what the older missionary had to say.

Moffat continued. 'There are vast areas north of where we work. And I have sometimes seen, in the light of the morning sun, the smoke of a thousand villages where no missionary has ever been.'

There was silence between the two men as David's mind took in the enormity of what he was hearing.

'What's the use of my waiting for the end of the opium war so that I can go to China?' he asked, not really expecting an answer. 'I will go at once to Africa instead.'

So it was that on 8th December 1840, David Livingstone boarded a ship that would carry him all the way to South Africa. Safely packed in his luggage was a box containing the first 500 copies of the New Testament in the Tswana language.

When Livingstone left for Africa, the Moffats thought that it would not be long until they would be following him. However, their circumstances changed and it wasn't until 30th January 1843 that they set sail once again for Cape Town, arriving two months and eleven days later.

'It would be much quicker by steamship,' Ann said, after some weeks at sea.

Her father smiled. 'You know, Ann, I seem to remember you saying that last time!'

'Do you believe that steam ships are a safe way of travelling now?' she asked.

'Of course I do,' said Robert. 'When I was a boy I thought the *Charlotte Dundas* was just a dream ship, but now I accept that steam is the way forward. Perhaps next time we go back to Britain we'll go on a ship powered by steam.'

It was Ann's turn to smile. 'I'm sure it will be,' she teased. 'You didn't go back for twenty-two years, so your next visit won't be until 1865 and you'll be seventy years old then!'

She was nearer the truth than either of them realised!

Because of a long stay in Cape Town and then a longer stay in Algoa Bay waiting for their luggage to arrive, the Moffats didn't reach Kuruman until December, nearly a year after leaving Britain. They were met 150 miles from home by David Livingstone, who had ridden out to greet them.

'My mother would have been proud of that young man,' Robert said to his wife, when they were alone late that night.

'Why?' wondered Mary.

'Well, she was determined to teach her sons as well as her daughters to sew, and David is wearing a suit that he made himself,' he explained.

Mary laughed. 'He's done more than you have then!'

Giving her a hug, Robert said, 'I've never needed to. You are so good at sewing!'

Once back at Kuruman the work began again. But some things were different. For instance, Mary, the oldest Moffat daughter, was now a young woman and she started work teaching in the school's infant class. Robert was soon up to date with what had happened while they'd been away.

'All the Tswana New Testaments have been distributed,' David told him. 'As I was instructed not to give them away if people could afford to buy them, many were exchanged for sheep or goats.'

Moffat approved of that, but he wanted to be sure that those who were really poor had not had to pay.

'Absolutely not!' he was assured. 'And children in the school didn't have to pay either.'

'That's good,' approved Robert. 'If they get into the habit of reading God's Word when they are children, we can look for great blessings as they grow up. But we'll need to order more now.'

More New Testaments were ordered, Robert paying for 2,000 of them himself! Having done the translation work, he was determined that as many Tswana people as could read should have one. And those who couldn't read should be taught and then have their own New Testament. Nobody was outside of his dream of what could happen in Kuruman!

* * *

Robert and Mary settled down once again to their work. From then on he was mostly kept busy with translating the rest of the Bible. She continued to teach her own children and the village women too, as well as taking sewing classes and even running a little shop! Meanwhile the new young missionary had his own ideas and they were not always instantly approved.

'I think we should train Tswana Christians as Bible teachers and then send them out as missionaries to their own people,' suggested David Livingstone. 'The mission has been here for twenty-five years and nobody has ever tried that. Only missionaries from overseas have travelled to the faraway villages to tell them about Jesus. But I'm sure Tswana people would learn better from other Tswana than from us.'

Robert Moffat and the other missionaries were rather worried about that. It's not always easy to see new ways of doing things when you've set up the old ways. It took eight years, and they must have seemed to be long years to David, before the senior missionaries began to act on his suggestion.

Those eight years were not lost. In fact, for two people in particular that was a very special time. They were David Livingstone and young Mary Moffat. On his travels David had an unfortunate meeting with a lion and his right arm was badly damaged in the encounter. Having gone back to Kuruman to recover, he discovered that Mary was a very kind and efficient nurse. To cut a long story short, they fell in love and were married. The Livingstones moved to Chonwane, around 250 miles from Kuruman, and started a new work there.

Travelling 250 miles today takes several hours by car, bus, train or plane but none of those had been invented in the 1840s. Although Robert was unable to make the trip because of his work, Mary Moffat and their three younger children travelled by the rattling and rumbling, clattering and trundling ox wagon all the way to Chonwane and back to visit the Livingstone branch of family.

'We saw thousands of wild animals,' one of the children wrote, as they travelled. 'There were dainty little steenboks, lordly elands, fantastic gnus, huge buffaloes and giraffes in procession.'

What a lot they had to tell their father when they returned a few weeks later.

Old Friends

In the years that followed most of Robert's time was spent translating the Old Testament into Tswana. Sometimes he would spend a whole day working on one verse trying to get the meaning exactly right. From time to time he needed a real break from that work and he had one in 1854. The London Missionary Society wanted the Moffats to return to Britain again, but he decided to visit his old friend King Moselekatse instead.

Loading his wagon with all that he needed for the journey still left some space and that was filled with supplies for David Livingstone.

'I wish we knew what was happening with David,' Mary said, as her husband was preparing to leave. 'All we know is that he went to work among the people groups along the Zambese, but we don't even know now if he's alive or dead.'

'I've no doubt I'll hear news of him while I'm away,' replied Robert. 'Let's just pray that it will be good news.'

Robert's journey was a long one and it was more than three weeks before he arrived in Moselekatse's kraal. And here is what he found, as he wrote it down later.

'On turning round, there Moselekatse sat – how changed! The vigorous, active and nimble chief of the Ndebele, now old, sitting on a skin, lame in his feet, unable to walk or even to stand.'

When the two men saw each other, tears rolled down Moselekatse's cheeks. He was so very pleased to see his friend again. Moffat recognised what was wrong with the King and treated him. What joy there was among the Ndebele to see him up and walking once again. For three months Robert and Moselekatse enjoyed each other's company, with the missionary often talking to his friend about the Lord Jesus.

When Robert prepared to leave and the King recognised that they had to part, Moselekatse had a plan.

'I know you have to go,' he said, 'but I am going to come with you for part of the way.'

As they travelled, a suitable place was found to leave the supplies brought for David Livingstone. They were placed on a little island in the Zambese and a roof was built over them. Amazingly David found them when he next passed that way some months later!

Eventually Robert and Moselekatse could not put off their parting any longer.

'I have not had time to show you enough kindness,' Moselekatse told his friend.

'Kindness!' replied Moffat. 'You have overwhelmed me with kindness. Now I leave you with my heart bursting with thankfulness.'

And that was how they parted.

* * *

Two years later the London Missionary Society hatched a plan for the Moffats, even though Robert was by then sixty-two years old. They wanted him to move to the Ndebele people, taking two other missionaries with him, and to stay there for a year and then leave the other two to continue the work. Moffat knew that King Moselekatse would be really pleased to see him again although he wasn't sure what he would think about the other missionaries. However, as he had finished the huge job of translating the Old Testament into Tswana, Robert decided it was the time to go. Remembering how important it was to the Ndebele to do things in the right way, he set off first to discuss the matter with the King. Moffat knew he couldn't just arrive with strangers and expect them to be welcome.

After his usual wonderful reception in Moselekatse's kraal, Robert explained the plans to his friend.

'I don't want other missionaries working here with my people,' the King announced. 'You know we had some from America before and that didn't work out well.'

Robert talked to him, explained to him, pled with him and prayed a great deal about the matter. Eventually his friend agreed that the other missionaries could come but only if Robert stayed with them.

When he returned to Kuruman, Moffat heard good news about the Livingstones.

'They are going to the Zambese,' he was told, 'and they are visiting Cape Town before they go.'

Discussions were held and it was agreed that the Moffats should leave the mission station and go to Cape Town to see the family. How they looked forward to seeing their daughter Mary again and to meeting their grandchildren. And there was an added bonus to this trip. Their own son, John, who had been in Britain training to be a missionary, was on board a ship for South Africa that would arrive while they were there! John was going to work with the Ndebele.

'Surely,' thought Robert, 'King Moselekatse will welcome my own son among his people.'

In July 1859 the oxen were once again pulling wagons towards the Ndebele people but some of the oxen became ill, and then others, and then still others.

'They've obviously caught something that's spreading among them,' Robert said. 'And we can't risk taking a disease to the Ndebele. Their animals might catch it and they could lose them all.'

It was agreed not to continue with beasts that were most likely infectious and a message was sent to the King explaining the problem and asking him to send oxen to take the wagons on their way.

When the runner came back with his reply, Robert was amazed and disappointed.

'He says that we've to go on using our own oxen and if the disease spreads to his ones, we won't be blamed for it as this was his decision.'

'But we can't do that,' John Moffat said. 'It's far too risky.'

Once again a runner was sent to the King, explaining that the disease was infectious and his animals could all catch it and die. An even more surprising message came back.

'I understand the danger,' said King Moselekatse, 'and you are right not to bring your oxen near mine. So I am sending warriors to drag your wagons instead.'

'Warriors!' said Robert and John together. 'Warriors dragging our wagons!'

Sure enough the warriors came, bringing some oxen with them.

'Thanks goodness for the oxen,' said the missionaries.

But the warriors explained that they were there to haul the wagons and the oxen were for eating!

Eventually the warriors got themselves harnessed to the wagons and for ten days there were cries of, 'A strong pull! A long pull! And a pull altogether!' But for all their strong pulls, and for all their long pulls, and for all their pulls together they were getting nowhere quickly. In ten days they had only gone a very short distance. The King eventually got the message and oxen were sent for the job and Robert and his companions eventually reached his kraal. Settling the new missionaries with the Ndebele people was not easy or quick, but eventually the work was started and grew.

Over the years the London Missionary Society had asked the Moffats to return to Britain for a year of recovery from all their hard work, and now it was suggested that it was time for them to go home for good.

'But Kuruman is our home,' they said to each other. 'We're not at home in Britain.'

Not only were they not at home in Britain, but several of their children were in Africa as missionaries and that's where grandchildren were being born to them. Despite all these things, it was agreed that they should sail once again across the seas to England.

'There's work for us to do there too,' Mary said. 'We'll tell Christians about the needs of the people in Africa and God will call other missionaries to come out and continue the work.'

'That certainly happened last time we were in Britain,' Robert agreed, 'or David Livingstone would have been a missionary in China rather than Africa.'

The decision having been taken, the elderly couple prepared for their departure.

It was Sunday 20th March, 1870, and it was the Moffats' last service in the church at Kuruman. There were many tears and many memories shared. Five days later, on the Friday, Robert and Mary climbed into their wagon and started on the eight-week long trek to Port Elizabeth. From there they sailed on the steamship *Roman* to Cape Town.

'Ann will be pleased to know that I've trusted myself to a steamship at last,' thought Robert, as they neared Cape Town.

And it was another steamship, the *Norseman* that took them to England.

'It's over fifty years since I left for Africa,' he thought, when they landed at Southampton. 'And I'll not set foot on that lovely land ever again.'

He was right.

As Robert and Mary moved from place to place they were welcomed as celebrities by Christians who had heard about them for years. Their stories about Africa and Africans were eagerly listened to wherever they went.

'Tell us about Chief Moselekatse,' some asked, who had heard Robert speak about his friend on his previous visit home.

Moffat would stroke his long white beard and talk for however long anyone wanted to listen. For he and his wife never grew tired of telling people about their friends in South Africa.

Less than a year after returning to Britain, Mary took ill and died.

'For fifty-three years I have had her to pray for me,' Robert said. And how he missed her prayers.

'How lonely I feel,' he wrote to a friend. And if it had not been for Jeanie (his daughter, who looked after him), it would have been even lonelier.

Despite his sad loss, it wasn't long before Robert Moffat was back to work as a missionary speaker, and he spent hours at his study desk.

'What are you doing?' Jeanie asked, finding him surrounded by papers.

'I'm rechecking the Tswana Old Testament before it goes off to print,' answered her father. 'I must get it right.'

'And he did' exclaimed his daughter, a few years later, as she held one of the precious printed copies.

'He spent his life and strength in working for the Lord and, for Africa. He was a lovely father and though he died in this cold country, his thoughts and prayers were always in his homeland. His big, brave heart was always for Africa.'

About the Author

Irene Howat is a Scot with a passion for books, whether reading them, writing them or choosing them to give as gifts. She also has a passion to share her Christian faith through the written word, especially with children. Having written over thirty books for boys and girls, she now has her own web-based story club which can be found at www.story-a-month-club.org.uk.

Writing hasn't been the only thing that has kept Irene busy. She supported her husband Angus in his ministry in Argyll until he retired, and they brought up three daughters. Two grandchildren now provide them with a great deal of joy and amusement.

For nearly ten years Irene has been Chairman of the Scottish Fellowship of Christian Writers and she has edited the Free Church of Scotland's monthly children's magazine since 1996.

As well as writing, Irene enjoys drawing, water-colour painting, photography, spending time with friends and watching DVDs of old detective films. There are always poetry books beside her chair and the best thumbed of them are by Evangeline Paterson.

Robert Moffat Timeline

1795	Robert Moffat born at Ormiston, East Lothian, Scotland.
1799	Explorer Mungo Park wrote 'Travels in the Interior of Africa'.
1801	Great Britain and Ireland become the United Kingdom.
1809	Robert started work as a gardener.
1810	Food was canned for the first time.
1813	Robert moved to Cheshire in England to work as a gardener there.
1814	Part of London was the first place to be lit by gas.
1815	Humphrey Davy invented a lamp that miners could use underground.
1816	Robert Moffat sailed as a missionary to South Africa.
1816	David Brewster invented the kaleidoscope.
1818	The Atlantic was crossed by a steamship for the first time.
1819	Mary joined Robert in South Africa and they were married.
1821	The population of the US reached 9.6 million.

1821	The Moffat's first child, Mary, was born. She later married David Livingstone.
1823	Charles Babbage made a calculating machine.
1825	The world's first passenger train ran from Stockton to Darlington in England.
1826	The first railway tunnel was opened between Liverpool and Manchester.
1829	Robert's first converts were baptised.
1830	There were twenty-six steam cars on the streets of London.
1839-43	The Moffats spent time in Britain.
1840	David Livingstone went to South Africa.
1843	There were 436,000 slaves in Cuba.
1851	The sewing machine was invented.
1863	Roller skating was introduced to America.
1870	Robert and Mary Moffat returned to Britain.
1871	Mary died.
1871	There was a great fire in Chicago.
1876	Alexander Graham Bell invented the telephone.
1879	Australian frozen meat sold in London.
1883	Robert Moffat died.

Thinking Further Topics

1. How it all Began
Robert and his brothers and sisters were brought up in an ordinary home yet he became a very famous missionary. Do you realise that God grows great people in ordinary families? That is how great a God he is. Ask God to help you to grow up to love him and serve him all of your life.

2. A Very Early Start
While Robert was still a young teenager he had to learn to work very hard. Jesus was brought up in a carpenter's home and he too would have learned hard work. Sometimes we give the impression that only brain work is worthwhile and we forget that God also wants us to work with our hands and get them dirty too.

3. All Change!
God brought about big changes in Robert's life. He went from being a gardener in England with a girl he loved to being a stranger in South Africa dreaming about her. Do you find change difficult? When changes happen in the Christian's life, we should remember that God's plans never fail. Look up Jeremiah 29:11 and think about it.

4. On the Move

Robert really offended a farmer by expecting him to bring his servants/slaves in for a Christian service. The farmer didn't really see them as people. How do you think about those who are at the bottom of the social heap? Are they 'the poor' or poor people? Are they 'beggars' or homeless people. Are they 'criminals' or people in prison?

5. Burning Hoofs

As Robert travelled some of the people he met tried to scare him by telling him terrible stories about Africaner. If you read the Christian press today you'll find some scary stories about what is happening to Christians in some parts of the world. The Christian life isn't easy; God never says that it will be. Ask him to help you to face the future, fears and all.

6. Namaqualand at Last!

The work at Africaner's kraal wasn't helped because relationships with the previous missionary were rather difficult. Do you think that Christians always get on well together? Of course they don't! But how should those who believe in Jesus deal with differences of opinion? Someone has said that it's not possible to hate someone and pray for them at the same time. Think about that.

7. On the Trail

How did you think Africaner felt as he and Robert neared Cape Town? Although Africaner was now a Christian, he had been an outlaw and might have to face punishment for the things he had done. Christians are forgiven all their sins in the eyes of God, but sometimes we have to bear consequences here on earth. Not all are treated as generously as Africaner was.

8. Good News!

When Robert heard that Mary was on her way to South Africa, he must have wanted to tell his mission leaders that he didn't want to go on their tour, he wanted to wait to welcome Mary. Why did he not do that? Was he right to go? How did God make it possible for him to be there to meet Mary when she arrived?

9. The Eight-day Loaf

Imagine how the missionary felt when he'd put so much work into making his bread only to have it stolen. What words do you think would describe his feelings? Do you think he felt kindly towards the villagers? What would have happened to his Christian witness had be raged and fumed and accused people of theft? Is it ever helpful to react like that?

10. Wars and more Wars

Robert helped the villagers when they were threatened and under attack. He also helped members of the enemy's people who were in trouble. Whose side was he on? Is it right to become involved in combat? Or should Christians be pacifists and not take part in conflicts at all?

11. Tswana in Print

Robert spent much of his time translating God's Word into Tswana. Why is it important that people can read the Bible in their own language? Why did Robert decide that he should learn the language himself? But there is no point in having a Bible in your own language if you don't read it. Do you read your Bible every day? It is God's way of speaking to you.

12. Chief Moselekatse

Moselekatse and Robert were friends for a very long time, but we never hear of the King becoming a Christian. Does that mean that Robert failed as a missionary? Should Christians have friends who don't believe in Jesus or should they just have friends who believe as they do?

13. Singing ABC

For many years Robert, Mary and their family lived a long way from a doctor. But, when they really needed a doctor, one was there and Mary's life was saved. Can you think of a time in your life when God has provided something or someone in an unexpected way? Think back over Robert's story for other examples of God being right there for his people.

14. Home from Home

It was more than twenty years between Robert and Mary leaving the UK and going back. What things were different in their families? Would there have been differences in other things too? Pray for missionaries who are separated from their families for years at a time, especially for their children who have to get to know grandparents, uncles, aunts and cousins all over again each time they go home.

15. 'My Name is David Livingstone'

David Livingstone thought God wanted him to go to China and decided that he should go to South Africa instead after speaking to Robert Moffat. Do you listen to older Christian people and take their opinions seriously? They have years of experience of serving the Lord and they are well worth listening to.

16. Old Friends

After serving the Lord in Africa for decades, Robert and Mary returned to the UK. Soon afterwards Mary became ill and died. What did Robert say he would miss very much indeed? Do you pray for those you love? When you say you will pray for someone, do you always remember to do so? Some years later Robert died too. Where do Christians go when they die? Read Revelation 21:3-4 to discover a little bit about the wonders and joys of heaven.

HEARTS AND HANDS
by Mindy and Brandon Withrow

Let history come to life – just the way it should do! Read the stories of the gifted preachers and justice fighters who led the 1st & 2nd Great Awakenings in the 18th and 19th centuries. Meet the American preacher who started a national revival in his tiny church. Spend time with the wealthy English politician and the former American slave woman who helped abolish slavery in their countries. Get to know the missionaries who built lasting Christian communities in China, India, and Africa. For the first 1700 years of the church, God's people had worked to define Christian teachings and secure their freedom to worship. Now they began to see, in a new way, how the power of the gospel should change their feelings both toward Jesus and their fellow human beings. Extra features look deeper into issues such as social reform, the French and American Revolutions, and the rise of Protestant Denominations.

ISBN: 978-1-84550-288-1

TRAILBLAZER SERIES

CHRISTIAN FOCUS PUBLICATIONS

Christian Focus | Christian Heritage | CF4K | Mentor

Christian Focus Publications publishes books for adults and children under its four main imprints: Christian Focus, CF4K, Mentor and Christian Heritage. Our books reflect our conviction that God's Word is reliable and Jesus is the way to know him, and live for ever with him.

Our children's publication list includes a Sunday School curriculum that covers pre-school to early teens, and puzzle and activity books. We also publish personal and family devotional titles, biographies and inspirational stories that children will love.

If you are looking for quality Bible teaching for children then we have an excellent range of Bible stories and age-specific theological books.

From pre-school board books to teenage apologetics, we have it covered!

Find us at our web page: www.christianfocus.com

CF4•K
Because you're never
too young to know Jesus